iPhone Design
Award-Winning Projects

Chris Dannen

Apress®

iPhone Design Award-Winning Projects

ISBN-13 (pbk): 978-1-4302-7235-9

ISBN-13 (electronic): 978-1-4302-7234-2

Printed and bound in the United States of America 9 8 7 6 5 4 3 2 1

Trademarked names may appear in this book. Rather than use a trademark symbol with every occurrence of a trademarked name, we use the names only in an editorial fashion and to the benefit of the trademark owner, with no intention of infringement of the trademark.

President and Publisher: Paul Manning
Lead Editors: Clay Andres
Developmental Editor: Douglas Pundick
Technical Reviewer: Joachim Bondo
Editorial Board: Clay Andres, Steve Anglin, Mark Beckner, Ewan Buckingham, Gary Cornell, Jonathan Gennick, Jonathan Hassell, Michelle Lowman, Matthew Moodie, Duncan Parkes, Jeffrey Pepper, Frank Pohlmann, Douglas Pundick, Ben Renow-Clarke, Dominic Shakeshaft, Matt Wade, Tom Welsh
Coordinating Editor: Kelly Moritz
Copy Editor: Tracy Brown Collins
Compositor: MacPS, LLC
Indexer: BIM Indexing and Proofreading Services
Artist: April Milne
Cover Designer: Anna Ishchenko

Distributed to the book trade worldwide by Springer-Verlag New York, Inc., 233 Spring Street, 6th Floor, New York, NY 10013. Phone 1-800-SPRINGER, fax 201-348-4505, e-mail orders-ny@springer-sbm.com, or visit http://www.springeronline.com.

For information on translations, please e-mail info@apress.com, or visit http://www.apress.com.

Apress and friends of ED books may be purchased in bulk for academic, corporate, or promotional use. eBook versions and licenses are also available for most titles. For more information, reference our Special Bulk Sales–eBook Licensing web page at http://www.apress.com/info/bulksales.

The information in this book is distributed on an "as is" basis, without warranty. Although every precaution has been taken in the preparation of this work, neither the author(s) nor Apress shall have any liability to any person or entity with respect to any loss or damage caused or alleged to be caused directly or indirectly by the information contained in this work.

Contents at a Glance

Contents

About the Authors

 **Chris Dannen** is a writer specializing in technology and innovation. He writes primarily for *FastCompany* magazine and Bnet.com, where he covers software, mobile technology, Web, mapping and all things Apple. He is also co-author of *Google Voice For Dummies* (Wiley, 2009). Chris received his BA from the University of Virginia and lives in the Williamsburg section of Brooklyn, NY.

About the Technical Reviewer

Joachim Bondo has developed software for three decades, from programmable calculators in the late '70s before computers were commonly available, to now the iPhone.

After releasing Deep Green, his critically acclaimed chess application, on the App Store, Joachim has contributed his excellent taste and insight on good user interface design to several Apress titles: *iPhone Games Projects, iPhone Advanced Projects, iPhone User Interface Design Projects*, and now *iPhone Design Award-Winning Projects*.

Acknowledgments

A great deal of gratitude is due to all the developers who sat for interviews in order to contribute to this book. Their patience, expertise and colorful explanations make this book what it is.

Special thanks to the developers who answered my incessant questions with extra detail, and took the time to explain ancillary concepts, code and hypotheticals at great length: Jonathan Wegener, Loren Brichter, Brandon Walkin and AJ of Marketcircle; Dave Witonsky for his enthusiasm and Marco Arment for one giant cup of green tea.

Thanks also to Clay Andres for his perennial guidance, and Kelly Moritz, Douglas Pundick, Tracy Brown Collins, and Joachim Bondo for their hard work and careful consideration. Many thanks also to Austin Carr, whose quick transcriptions saved me from the woes of carpal tunnel.

Finally, thanks to my editors at *FastCompany*, Noah Robischon and Lynne d Johnson particularly, for accommodating the crazed schedule I adopted while writing this book.

Introduction

Readme

This is a book about building apps with good design, parsimonious code and aesthetic appeal on the Apple iPhone and iPod Touch. At times, this book references code and give sample projects; other times, it delves into interaction and visual design. It doesn't take a CS doctorate to appreciate or even understand, but some familiarity with programming is assumed.

Who is this book for?

Lots of people. Mac developers looking to do a killer iPhone app might want to know the hard-won lessons or philosophies of others; iPhone hackers looking to step up their game might be trying to figure out how much to emulate Apple. Anyone who appreciates a success story will hopefully enjoy this book, but it's also inspirational.

How technical is it?

Parts of this book assumes basic knowledge of C or other object-oriented programming languages. In some cases, we reference specific Apple frameworks and interface guidelines. It will also help to be familiar with the Apple environment, from the quirks of the App Store to technologies inside OS X.

How were these interviewees chosen?

The five core chapters of this book are based on a series of interviews with five of the 2009 winners of Apple Design Awards (ADAs) for the iPhone. MLB.com, the makers of the sixth ADA winner, MLB.com at Bat, did not consent to be interviewed for this book in order to protect their intellectual property.

The remaining six developers interviewed for this book were chosen by its writer and editors because they buttressed some of the discussions in the core chapters, or because they provided a contrasting philosophy to another developer in the book. It was important not only that these six apps use Apple frameworks competently, but that they also smartly navigated the App Store, its frenetic marketplace, and its fickle economy.

Speaking of money: this book also aims to address the philosophies behind monetizing (or not monetizing) an app. How do I set an optimal price? Should my app be free? How about the upgrade? What are the risks of in-app purchasing? It's not as much fun as talking about code or UI, but sometimes monetization means the difference between designing the app you want, or compromising to cover your overhead.

Lastly, this book tries to garner thoughts and opinions from developers building a wide variety of software. Several of the apps highlighted herein are tied into desktop companion apps or websites; others discuss the construction and revision of sequels. Some of the developers themselves aim to startup iPhone-only shops, while some are veteran Mac developers or new-to-Apple developers looking to experiment. But they're all motivated by a single question: how do I build a better iPhone app in concept and in practice?

Chris Dannen

Innovating Beyond Apple's Design Standards, While Maintaining Apple's Logic for Consistency, Clarity, and Usability

With over 100,000 apps in the App Store, how have Facebook and Tweetie managed to rise above the rabble? Used by millions of iPhone owners and accessed just as often as many of Apple's native apps, both these social network clients wield incredible influence, not only over their users, but also over the way UI standards come to be accepted by the iPhone masses in general. These are no normal apps. They are apps that help make the platform.

Tweetie and Facebook are incredibly deep and beautifully-engineered pieces of software. The two are made for very different use--Tweetie is borne of singular purpose, while Facebook is evolving to be a Swiss Army app--but they are alike in one particular trait: personality. Both developers have crafted their vision of iPhone UI with stubborn confidence, but also even-handedness. Where they believe Apple has shown ingenuity, they pay competent homage. But where they believe Apple has lapsed, they gladly pick up the pace of innovation and carry it forward.

This is no small assumption on an Apple device, which, like other Apple products, has come to vaunt its remarkable ease of use and its long, careful development as the reasons for its success. Loren Brichter and Joe Hewitt, the developers featured in this section, don't seem worried. It's a combination of humility and precociousness that could only be called Jobsian.

Chapter 1

Tweetie

Developer name: Loren Brichter
Development Company: Atebits
Tags: Layout; Efficient Code; Workflow
URL: http://atebits.com

"I can't go into details because I think everything is under NDA for, like, the next 20 years," says Loren Brichter, the founder and sole developer at Philadelphia-based Mac shop atebits, and developer of Tweetie (Figure 1–1). He's talking about the top-secret program he worked on at Apple: the iPhone.

Figure 1–1. *Tweetie's innovative UI won it a cult following.*

He stayed for a year—the most exciting year of his life, by his own account. But having grown up on Manhattan's Upper West Side and gone to Tufts University in Boston, Brichter was a Right Coast kid and he couldn't stay away. He moved back East, sat down, and did the only thing he knew how to do: he wrote a Mac app.

"My first product was a little drawing app called Scribbles," he says. "It kept me a live, it made a little bit of money, but it wasn't hugely successful." He was good with Cocoa and OpenGL; the projects that had gotten him hired at Apple were an iTunes visualizer and a soft-body physics simulator. Once assigned to the iPhone project, he had worked in the guts of Cocoa, at the UIKit level and below. He was a programmer's programmer. So it was no surprise that when he first signed up for Twitter in November 2007, he was more or less disgusted by the brevity of 140-character tweets. "I signed up, used it for five minutes, and decided: this is stupid," he says.

It would be a year before he started using it again, to keep up with the tweets of tech pundit John Gruber. Why? "Gruber is interesting guy," Brichter says. He found there were actually lots of other interesting guys on Twitter. "People joke about Twitter, that it's stupid and superficial," Brichter says. "And if you follow superficial people, it's superficial. But if you follow interesting people, it's interesting."

A Billion Bad Twitter Apps

It was around the same time that his Verizon Wireless contract expired and he finally got an iPhone. He started scouring the App Store. "I realized there are no good Twitter apps," he recalls. "But there are a billion bad ones." He figured he could probably write a better app. "What triggered me to do it? I was playing with Twitterific, which I used, and everybody used. I thought: I wonder why the scrolling is so slow? I wonder if I can make it faster." In an hour, he had built a prototype of a list of fast-scrolling tweets. Then, after a two-week paroxysm of coding, he had built Tweetie, shown in Figure 1–1, which is as of this writing the most popular mobile Twitter client on any platform, and the most popular Twitter app for iPhone.

Brichter attributes Tweetie's meteoric rise in popularity to a cocktail of luck, quality programming, and some well-timed publicity. But what really lives at the core of his success—and Tweetie's—is an absolute intolerance for mediocrity. "I have a shit-list of Twitter apps that just drive me insane," he says. "Apple lays out all these guidelines and conventions about how to write an iPhone app, and these developers basically looked at them and did the exact opposite in every single case."

He's not looking for perfection, however—just parsimony. If it's one concept of design and interaction that gets Brichter excited, it's economy of energy, be it in actual usage scenarios or in software development. Ask him what aggravated him about the existing selection of Twitter apps back in November of 2008, when he wrote Tweetie, and he doesn't talk about their ugliness or their complexity. Even the slowness that bugged him in Twitterific is merely a symptom of flawed thinking. "The problem isn't with how the other apps used Twitter's API, it's with the way they interacted with the iPhone OS," he says. "Either they were doing something completely custom, or completely wrong." His antipathy wasn't even aimed at Twitterific, though it was the immediate catalyst for

Tweetie. "To tell you the truth, I didn't have a lot of beef with Twitterific," he says. "They were the ADA winner from the year before, and everyone loved the app. It just didn't jibe with the way I used Twitter."

It's not that Brichter is a loyal Apple devotee, either; he has beef with plenty of the native apps. "On the SMS app, the 'Send' button is right next to the keyboard," he quibbles, "so you hit it accidentally. There's no reason they couldn't have put it up in the nav bar." Mail too was a cautionary tale for Tweetie. "Everything in Mail is twice as many taps [as with Tweetie]. You have the account list, then the folder list, and then you get into the message list," he says. "I want to be able to go into an inbox with one tap, not two or three." (Figure 1–2 shows the first tweet feed prototype; Figure 1–3 shows a second iteration.)

Figure 1–2. *The first Tweetie fast-scrolling prototype.*

Figure 1–3. *Another scrolling iteration, this one more iChat-inspired.*

The atebits way of using something, distilled, is the pursuit the path of least resistance. "I got lucky, because the way I originally wrote Tweetie made sense in terms of how you should interact with a Twitter app," he says. His idea of how a user "should" use Twitter is based the navigation Apple Mail, made better: each tap in a tweet's menu pushes you rightward into a deeper folder. That's how Tweetie manages to pack in Recent Tweets, Search @, Following, Followers, and Block/Unblock without a mess of buttons or oddball menus. "It doesn't seem complicated—that's how every Twitter app should work," he says. "But yet that's not how Twitter apps work."

The most popular functions aren't made available through more buttons, or more menus—just swipe, as if you're deleting an email or a text, and you have the ability to star, @reply, or see the profile of the user whose tweet you're investigating (though you can also do this by clicking a tweet, if you're not aware of the shortcut). "My philosophy was: don't fight the framework," he says. "UI Kit APIs are so insanely beautiful that you can pick them up super-fast, even if you don't know how to program. It provides all this awesome functionality, but all these other apps do things their own custom way. But if you just embrace the UI Kit philosophy, you can build an app like Tweetie really fast." (Figure 1–1 shows the swipe shortcut.)

Easy for the ex-Apple iPhone wonk to say, right? Well, sort of. "At Apple I didn't do any app stuff except some performance tuning for other teams—making apps faster, doing some fancy looking transitions. I didn't really have any app building experience at all, so when I sat down to start writing Tweetie, I was learning the process from scratch."

The Minimalist Flourish

While Brichter might have a thing for parsimony, the fine-tuning he did during his year at Apple is readily apparent in both Tweetie and Scribbles in a handful of beautiful actions. Make a command—a new document or tweet, or the preferences pane—and the window slips out from under the menu bar with a flourish, in a kind of reverse-genie effect inspired by the dock. Things in both apps move uncannily fast; even on a dual-core Macs where waiting is a rarity, the file browser practically rockets out of a tweet's title bar. Atebits apps are compact, purpose-built and deceptively robust, like race-tuned Mini Coopers of the Cocoa realm. (Figure 1–4 shows a tweet in the making, using Tweetie for Mac.)

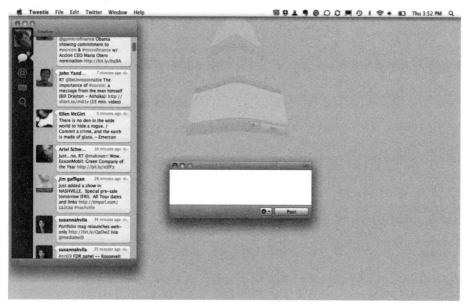

Figure 1–4. *Tweetie for Mac, which uses the same codebase as Tweetie 2 for iPhone, contains subtle, rapid animations.*

Economy of design is often accompanied by minimalism, and Brichter's work style is fittingly Spartan. He doesn't use Interface Builder; all of Tweetie versions 1 and 2 were built programmatically in Xcode. And unlike most of the Mac developers in this book, uses just one machine and just one screen. "A few months ago I got a 17-inch MacBook Pro, and my Mac Pro has been in storage ever since," he says. It took Brichter just five days of coding to build the Twitter-iPhone core inside Tweetie 1, a few days doing the user interface, and a few more in the hands of beta testers; the whole app weighed in at 30,000 lines of code.

It is perhaps because of Twitter's straightforwardness that Brichter's Tweetie project makes for such an excellent example for developers. Unlike most apps, Tweetie has the benefit (and the onus) of an extant paradigm: the Web version of Twitter The extent to which Tweetie (or any Twitter iPhone app) succeeds is based largely on one question: how much additional cognitive load will it take me to use Twitter using this app instead of the Web?

To give Tweetie parity with the Web experience, Brichter first built in all the features an average user would want, but he didn't stop there; he lets power-users navigate reply chains, upload pictures to Twitpic.com, view trends, do searches, search nearby users using the phone's A-GPS, and even built a bookmarklet that users can deploy in mobile Safari to send links to Tweetie. In 1.2, the first major feature update of release, he added Instapaper support, landscape keyboard, image compression control for Twitpic uploads, those Mail-like swipe shortcuts, stock quote links, and the ability to forward direct messages to email (for more on Instapaper, see Chapter 13). If you're a Twitter Web user, you know that a whole lot of those features don't even appear anywhere on Twitter itself.

So features he had in spades—but having tons of features is often anathema to usability. Since it was Twitterific's slow scrolling that compelled him to build Tweetie in the first place, Brichter first set out to invent a new way the iPhone rendered its table cells. Most apps—in accordance Apple's own tutorials—force the phone to render a morass of subviews of labels and images, but Brichter's code pre-blends everything together using CoreGraphics. Once it renders that first frame, it hands one opaque static view over to CoreAnimation without the need to rely on the GPU to do any blending Brichter was so convinced that his fast-scrolling code was superior to Apple's that he posted a tutorial on his web site, where he makes his case: "If you think about what is happening in terms of overdraw, having one big view per table cell is a big win, because CoreAnimation will only touch a single given pixel on the screen once rather than multiple times (potentially, depending on how much overlap your old view hierarchy had)," he wrote.[1]

As with Tweetie, Brichter's sample project relies on just one class of object for everything: ABTableViewCell.h and ABTableViewCell.m. In Listing 1–1, he creates a sample list of words with a first- and last-name field in two separate fonts as in the Contacts app.

List 1–1. *Creating a first- and last-name field*

```
//
//  FirstLastExampleTableViewCell.m
//  FastScrolling
//
//  Created by Loren Brichter on 12/9/08.
//  Copyright 2008 atebits. All rights reserved.
//

#import "FirstLastExampleTableViewCell.h"
```

---

[1] http://blog.atebits.com/2008/12/fast-scrolling-in-tweetie-with-uitableview/

```
@implementation FirstLastExampleTableViewCell

@synthesize firstText;
@synthesize lastText;

static UIFont *firstTextFont = nil;
static UIFont *lastTextFont = nil;

+ (void)initialize
{
        if(self == [FirstLastExampleTableViewCell class])
        {
                firstTextFont = [[UIFont systemFontOfSize:20] retain];
                lastTextFont = [[UIFont boldSystemFontOfSize:20] retain];
                // this is a good spot to load any graphics you might be drawing in -
drawContentView:
                // just load them and retain them here (ONLY if they're small enough
that you don't care about them wasting memory)
                // the idea is to do as LITTLE work (e.g. allocations) in -
drawContentView: as possible
        }
}

- (void)dealloc
{
        [firstText release];
        [lastText release];
    [super dealloc];
}

// the reason I don't synthesize setters for 'firstText' and 'lastText' is because I
need to
// call -setNeedsDisplay when they change

- (void)setFirstText:(NSString *)s
{
        [firstText release];
        firstText = [s copy];
        [self setNeedsDisplay];
}

- (void)setLastText:(NSString *)s
{
        [lastText release];
        lastText = [s copy];
        [self setNeedsDisplay];
}

- (void)drawContentView:(CGRect)r
{
        CGContextRef context = UIGraphicsGetCurrentContext();

        UIColor *backgroundColor = [UIColor whiteColor];
        UIColor *textColor = [UIColor blackColor];

        if(self.selected)
```

```
        {
                backgroundColor = [UIColor clearColor];
                textColor = [UIColor whiteColor];
        }

        [backgroundColor set];
        CGContextFillRect(context, r);

        CGPoint p;
        p.x = 12;
        p.y = 9;

        [textColor set];
        CGSize s = [firstText drawAtPoint:p withFont:firstTextFont];

        p.x += s.width + 6; // space between words
        [lastText drawAtPoint:p withFont:lastTextFont];
}

@end
```

ABTableViewCell.m reads:

```
#import "ABTableViewCell.h"

@interface ABTableViewCellView : UIView
@end

@implementation ABTableViewCellView

- (void)drawRect:(CGRect)r
{
        [(ABTableViewCell *)[self superview] drawContentView:r];
}

@end



@implementation ABTableViewCell
```

ABTableViewCell.h reads:

```
#import <UIKit/UIKit.h>

// to use: subclass ABTableViewCell and implement -drawContentView:

@interface ABTableViewCell : UITableViewCell
{
        UIView *contentView;
}

- (void)drawContentView:(CGRect)r; // subclasses should implement

@end
```

RootConroller.m reads:

```
//
//  RootViewController.m
//  FastScrolling
//
//  Created by Loren Brichter on 12/9/08.
//  Copyright atebits 2008. All rights reserved.
//

#import "RootViewController.h"
#import "FastScrollingAppDelegate.h"
#import "FirstLastExampleTableViewCell.h"

@implementation RootViewController

- (void)viewDidLoad
{
        self.title = @"Fast Scrolling Example";
    [super viewDidLoad];
}

- (NSInteger)tableView:(UITableView *)tableView numberOfRowsInSection:(NSInteger)section
{
    return 100;
}

static NSString *randomWords[] = {
@"Hello",
@"World",
@"Some",
@"Random",
@"Words",
@"Blarg",
@"Poop",
@"Something",
@"Zoom zoom",
@"Beeeep",
};

#define N_RANDOM_WORDS (sizeof(randomWords)/sizeof(NSString *))

- (UITableViewCell *)tableView:(UITableView *)tableView
cellForRowAtIndexPath:(NSIndexPath *)indexPath
{
        static NSString *CellIdentifier = @"Cell";

        FirstLastExampleTableViewCell *cell = (FirstLastExampleTableViewCell
*)[tableView dequeueReusableCellWithIdentifier:CellIdentifier];
        if(cell == nil)
        {
                cell = [[[FirstLastExampleTableViewCell alloc]
initWithStyle:UITableViewCellStyleDefault reuseIdentifier:CellIdentifier] autorelease];
        }

        cell.firstText = randomWords[indexPath.row % N_RANDOM_WORDS];
        cell.lastText = randomWords[(indexPath.row+1) % N_RANDOM_WORDS];
```

```
        return cell;
}


- (void)tableView:(UITableView *)tableView didSelectRowAtIndexPath:(NSIndexPath
*)indexPath
{
        [tableView deselectRowAtIndexPath:indexPath animated:YES];
}

@end
```

In July 2009, almost eight months after Brichter posted his tutorial on the atebits blog, Apple updated their iPhone Reference Library to include his method as one of the suggested scrolling solutions, though as Brichter points out, it's the last suggested example as of this writing.[2]

Tweetie's scrolling, which Brichter is fond of calling "ridiculously fast," is technically a bug, because it doesn't save state between launches. And because of its speed, it conceals the true memory load the app presents the iPhone OS. "You'd be surprised—when you think of all the avatars you're loading while you're scrolling by, those take up memory," he says. Thanks to Shark and Instruments, memory management wasn't a burden, he says, but there's another lurking problem in Tweetie: its inline browser. "The biggest pain in the ass of iPhone development is using UIWebView," he says, "because that thing just sucks up memory like crazy." On 2G and 3G iPhones, he says, the browser taxes the phone so much that the OS frequently kills it, crashing the app. "You've gotta give Apple some credit, because they're doing something complex," he says of in-app browsing. "But it's the single biggest headache I ran into."

Tearing Down Tweetie

Twitter's API, while "quirky," didn't give him too much trouble, Brichter says, yet that didn't stop him from re-engineering the entire app during the development of Tweetie 2. "When I wrote Tweetie 1, I got a lot right, but I also got a lot wrong. At the UI level, there was a list of nit-picks that I had to address," he says. "But it was really just the code was a mess: I reimplemented stuff a few times." One example: because the regular Twitter API for retrieving tweets is different than the API for searching tweets, Brichter says he ended up with a lot of duplicated code behind the scenes. Building Tweetie for Mac, which he launched in spring of 2009 and is $19.95 through the atebits web site, he recoded the bulk of the app, which he subsequently began modifying to for use in Tweetie 2. He calls the new codebase BigBird. "Now it's all unified and pretty," he says.

---

[2] http://developer.apple.com/iphone/library/samplecode/TableViewSuite/index.html
[Apple Developer Account required.]

But Brichter doesn't characterize Tweetie 2 as the progeny of Tweetie for the desktop—in fact, it's actually the iPhone version that fathered the desktop iteration. As he told a Stanford University undergraduate computer science class in May 2009, just before winning an Apple Design Award, he actually mimicked the iPhone's UITableView controller on the Mac. "Once you feel the philosophy of [iPhone] view controllers flow through you, it's this really beautiful concept," he told the class. They chuckled at his sincerity, but remained rapt as he described something he calls ABTableViewController, the manifestation of his iPhone philosophy ported to Mac. Double-click on a tweet in Tweetie for Mac, and you see a tab view controller at work, as well as a sub-view controller, all of which are operating inside of a navigation controller. "It's this idea that you can have a ton of info and be able to delve into it without having to scroll across your screen," he told the class. "When you're looking at a tweet, you see the tweet details beneath. If you want to see user details, rather than sliding over to another screen—which would just be another view controller pushed onto the navigation controller stack—there's a little button that will slide down the tweet and reveal the information beneath it. But those are actually two separate view controllers," he says. "I have view controllers within view controllers within view controllers within navigation controllers." The result, he says, is a "beautiful hierarchy" that allows you to eschew the usual logic of presentation. The other result, of course, is a Twitter app that lives in a fraction of the screen space of TweetDeck and other popular desktop apps and flows through each of its functions with minimal buttons and menus.

Organic Marketing

Brichter says that Tweetie has taken over his life in the last year; he's still pulling 100-hour weeks developing updates and new versions. Still, there's a good reason he has the luxury of flying out to Stanford to guest lecture: he has spent almost no time doing marketing, and yet the sales keep rolling in.

The story of Tweetie's no-marketing marketing start with quality of the app itself. His sales began to climb at first only because of word of mouth—he had indeed succeeded in making something better than Twitterific, Twittelator, and Twitterfon, and word spread quickly (even though he says that in hindsight, his foray into the crowded Twitter iPhone app space was "batshit-insane." He also tweeted about the app to find beta testers, and when the first release dropped he had a ready audience who could retweet the announcement. After that, he added something he jokingly called "Popularity Enhancers," or project "PEE." It added fart sounds and a flashlight to Tweetie: features "meant to make fun of the App Store," he says. He also added a page to the atebits web site touting PEE with what can only be called unconventional salesmanship.[3] (Figures 1–5 and 1–6 show images he added to atebits.com to promote PEE.)

PEE is a collection of ever-growing technologies scientifically designed to enhance the size of that certain something … you guessed it: App Store sales!

---

[3] http://atebits.com/pee

Teams from around the globe have analyzed figures and come up with a secret formula for App Store success. I share these findings today, ABSOLUTELY FREE. Success is made up of: a FLASHLIGHT… and DIRTY WET FART SOUNDS!!!

Tweetie, the only app that bundles together these two incredible features FOR THE VERY FIRST TIME. Accept no imitations. Why buy a dedicated fart app AND a flashlight, when you can have BOTH, and get a TWITTER CLIENT along with it! Read on for more details…."

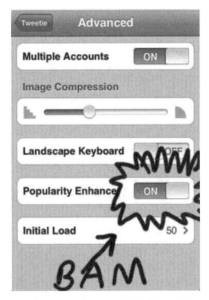

Figure 1–5. *A screenshot Brichter added to atebits' PEE web site.*

Figure 1–6. *Brichter's personification of Tweetie with PEE enabled, as pictured on atebits' PEE web site.*

Tech news sites like ArsTechnica picked up the PEE features; sales quintupled day-over-day. Then Apple decided to feature the app on its iTunes Store's opening screen. Even more sales. Then Apple did Brichter another favor: they rejected Tweetie update 1.3.

This wasn't Brichter's first rejection: they had rejected his initial submission because he used the open-book bookmarks icon as a "favorites" icon used to save searches. That was an easy fix: he changed the open-book icon to a star. The second rejection was more puzzling. At the time he submitted the update, one of the trending terms on Twitter was the "f*ckit list." Brichter says, "Apple saw the trending term, and they were like, 'No you can't have curse words in the app'." Others people picked up the rejection when Brichter tweeted about it, and sales of the app skyrocketed—even though the updated version in question wasn't in the app store yet. Brichter says that Apple acknowledged the error in judgment and resolved the issue within a day, but the publicity stuck and sales kept climbing. To date, Tweetie has reached as high as number six on Apple's overall list of paid apps, and has topped the social networking category. Brichter says he's not comfortable sharing revenue numbers, but sufficed to say it has made atebits a very, very viable company. (Figure 1–7 shows the relative sales boosts of each of Brichter's marketing events.)

The parts of Tweetie's marketing that Brichter actually orchestrated on purpose—project PEE, his announcement tweets—are examples of how economical thinking can keep a lone developer from over-extending himself. Instead of launching a web campaign or trying to contact journalists, Brichter simply did what he knew how to do: he wrote more Objective-C, and tried to make Tweetie more fun. When he wanted to get the word out, he found his audience where he knew they'd be: on Twitter. He didn't bother wasting time becoming an impromptu expert on app marketing; it just didn't promise much of a return. He let the journalists do their job by discovering him, and let the customers do what they like doing: suggest a cool new app to their friends. When sales began booming and Brichter began getting hundreds of emails a day on his customer service account, he responded similarly: he outsourced it to an Arizona-based software engineer named Ash Ponders.

The second installment of Brichter's no-marketing campaign, the Apple rejection, allowed him to benefit from a curious phenomenon: iPhone owners rebelling against the App Store by buying something as a show of solidarity through the App Store. So fickle and unpredictable has the app approval process become that users jumped at the opportunity to show support for an app they thought didn't get its fair shake. If there were an allegory for iPhone users' simultaneous love and hatred for their devices, the Tweetie rejection drew it out: iPhone owners love their devices, and few will stand idly by while a BlackBerry or Android fanboy tries to overstate its flaws. But they also feel suckered by AT&T, the U.S. iPhone service provider whose coverage and call-quality on the iPhone is famously unreliable, and by Apple, which sometimes acts paternalistic in their content-censoring. In the beginning, Apple was pickier about accepting only apps with consistent usability standards. "Now they're just rejecting stuff that's ridiculous—they rejected a dictionary app because there are curse words in it. They're rejecting all the wrong things," Brichter says. Still, plenty of Tweetie's less-capable competition slipped right through the process, even though they didn't follow any of Apple's interaction standards. "I guess Apple lightened up [on usability] because they realized people suck at UI and user experience," he theorizes. "I guess they wanted the numbers in the App Store; they wanted to be able to claim they had 50,000 apps, and they realized if they cracked down on crappy UI they wouldn't have those numbers."

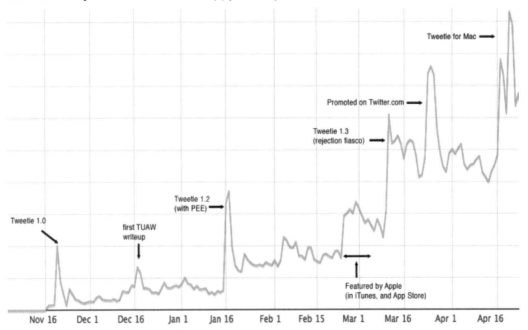

Figure 1–7. *Apple's rejection of Tweetie 1.3 provided one of Brichter's biggest sales boosts.*

Though Brichter says he didn't give Tweetie's pricing much thought ("I put work into this app, I may as well charge money for it," he says), he has received a powerful and profitable lesson in the economics of the App Store. "I think Apple was smart setting the limit at 99 cents, otherwise we'd have bidding down to like 5 cents or 10 cents for an app," he says. But by pricing his app at $2.99, instead of the one-dollar standard, Brichter is an example to developers that an app doesn't need to be bargain-bin cheap or free to make it into the top 10 list. "Honestly I think the right price depends on the app; there are certain kinds of apps that target the cheapo's. But who's your market? People with iPhones—people are spending tons of money on iPhones. The vast majority of those people have the extra money that they can spend 2 or 3 bucks on an app," he says.

Brichter's $2.99 price-point may also imply higher quality to shoppers. Since there's no way to preview or demo apps on the app store before buying, price may have become a valuable clue to worthiness; few developers would have the guts to put out a $2.99 app unless they expected five-star reviews. "I thought $2.99 was also within the range of impulse buy for most people. There wasn't really too much else out there competing with it, so people picked up on it," Brichter says. Contrary to many developers on the iTunes Store, Brichter thought a free version would cannibalize sales; because he had developed Tweetie with so little overhead, he didn't need to make an immediate play for market share. "The fact that I didn't release a free lite version probably helped the sales of the paid version," he says. "I don't want to sound sleazy, but there are some percentage of users who would have downloaded the free version, said this is good enough, and even if they were willing to spend three dollars, they wouldn't have spent it."

The key to app-pricing psychology, Brichter thinks, is getting customers over the decision to buy. "I think the barrier between zero and one dollar is huge," he says, "and the barrier between 99 cents and $2.99 is relatively small." For all the talk of "downward pressure" on app prices in the iTunes Store, Brichter says that many developers are leaving money on the table by going as low as possible. He has even considered going higher. "I'm not sure what the limit is: five, six, seven bucks? Then again, you could buy lunch for that," he says.

Brichter spent about half a year building Tweetie 2 for iPhone, inventing a variety of iPhone OS 3.0 features and modifying the slick new Tweetie core from the desktop version. The new version of Tweetie allows for in-app email composition: you can copy an entire threaded direct message conversation into an email, formatted in rich HTML. It also uses MapKit to plot nearby tweets and users, runs in landscape mode, and supports full persistence.

Tweetie 2

Brichter is perfectly aware that his apps live and die by users' whimsy, so he has taken big
risks to make Tweetie 2 a substantial improvement over its predecessor (shown in Figure 1–8). Unlike other iPhone apps, Twitter apps require very little informational investment from users. In apps like RunKeeper or iFitness, for example, users spend time logging their workouts; in Beejive, the instant-messaging app, they spend time adding accounts and buddies, and tweaking backgrounds or settings. But Twitter apps are comparatively plug-and-play. "There's no lock-in with Twitter clients," Brichter observes, "so if something comes out that's better, they'll use it. They just sign in and all their info is there." He's hoping that features like Tweetie's slick new navigation and hierarchy will keep users hooked, but all it takes is a sexier alternative to erode Tweetie's lead. "Tweetie is in a unique position where market share is meaningful," he says; since Twitter advertises which client a tweet comes from, the more mentions the better. Market share is so meaningful, in fact, that Brichter doesn't seem particularly concerned about piracy. Yes, there are copies of Tweetie on torrent sites, he concedes. "But that actually helps me because it increases Tweetie's user base."

Figure 1–8. *Tweetie 2, pictured on the left, drastically re-imagines profile viewing.*

Perhaps Tweetie 2's most drastic departure from Tweetie 1 is the dynamic navigation bar at the bottom of the screen. In versions 1.X, Tweetie's lower nav stayed anchored with all of "your stuff," as Brichter terms it, shown in Figure 1–1: tweets, mentions, messages, favorites, and the "more" button, all viewable in the home screen. In Tweetie 2, the bottom nav appears in several screens, but changes function; when you're viewing a user, the glossy black tabs change to apply to that user, no longer to your stuff. (Figure 1–9 shows the dynamic nav bar at work viewing one user's tweets.) Navigation is relegated to the top bar, which lets you dip in and out of directories.[4] That leaves the top navigation buttons to handle navigation when drilling deeper (or backing out into the main screen). The navigation that appears at the top of the screen varies based on the tab selected in the bottom navigation bar. In that respect, Tweetie for Mac and Tweetie for iPhone now share a logic. But that logic is contrary to what most iPhone users are used to; in most apps, the bottom nav stays static no matter where you go in the app, and when clicked, take the user upwards in the current directory. Brichter explains his rationale below:

> When you use UITabBarController, you are forced to have an application-global tab bar. This doesn't work in Tweetie 2.
>
> The "root" view in Tweetie 2 is the account list. Having an application-global tab bar at the bottom of this screen makes no sense (how can you switch between the Timeline and Mentions of... nothing?)
>
> Tapping on an account brings you to the "account details" screen. Within this screen you can switch between different "parts" of the selected account. You can view the account's Timeline, the account's Mentions, Messages, Drafts, etc.

---

[4] To read a contrasting take on Tweetie 2's dynamic navigation bar, check out Chapter 4.

This "level" in the hierarchy is appropriate for a tab bar. The tabs control the currently viewed "part" of that specific account.

One you tap on something within this level, you are directed into more detail views. When you tap on a tweet, bottom area morphs into toolbar with tweet-specific actions. When you view user details, the bottom area morphs into user-specific navigation tabs...you can view that specific user's recent tweets, mentions, favorites, and profile.

Having an application-global tab bar is extremely limiting. In Tweetie 2 I'm optimizing for navigation stack *depth*. By having a screen-specific bottom bar that morphs depending on current context you can expose a massive wealth of information without requiring the user to deal with excessive drill-down.

Apple doesn't do this. In fact, they don't recommend doing what I'm doing. While I think Tweetie 2 is a great example of an iPhone-ish iPhone app, I'm bucking the HIG because I think Apple's recommendations are too confining. A shallow app can get away with an application-global tab bar. A deep, rich app can't. And Tweetie 2 is deep.

The tricks in Tweetie 2 let you explore massive amounts of information without the tap...tap...tap of pushing tons of view controllers onto the navigation stack. As a quick example, say I'm looking at a tweet in my timeline. A user is asking the Twitterverse a question. I want to check out responses. I can swipe the tweet, tap the user details button, then tap the @ tab of the pushed user-details screen. I'm viewing the responses to this user from everyone, and I'm only a *single* view controller away from where I started.

```
Tweet list -> Recent user mentions
```

Without optimizing for navigation stack depth, imagine if I had to push a new view controller for each navigation action:

```
Tweet list -> Tweet details -> User details -> Recent user mentions
```

This stinks.

I don't use a normal tab bar in Tweetie 2 for these context-specific tab bars. I draw them with custom code. I wanted them to be familiar, but different enough that users didn't expect the standard application-global tabs.

I don't recommend everyone follow my lead. Twitter is *incredibly* rich with information. Chances are most other apps are shallow enough and will be good enough using an application-global tab bar or just simple drill-down.

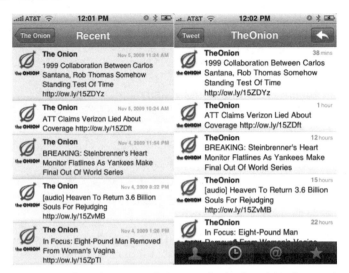

Figure 1–9. *Tweetie 2's dynamic lower navigation bar, right, changes depending on what the user views. In Tweetie 1, the lower navigation bar doesn't exist outside the home screen.*

Market Share

If ever there were a word that encapsulated Twitter, "market share" would be it. The company has no revenue stream and no discernible plans for one, even as profitable cottage industries sprout up around it. IPhone apps are only one slice: on the Web, users can sign up for EasyTweets for marketing, Twuffer for future-scheduled tweeting, Twittervision for real-time mapping, Tweetree for keeping track of @replies, Twtpoll for surveys, FollowFormation for who-to-follow suggestions ... the list burgeons. Since its inception in 2006, Twitter's singular goal has been earning users and stifling competitors—even before there were competitors to stifle. The service has an easy and robust API, and has been sure to let user ship grow unfettered, without any of the controlled growth or moderation users associate with Facebook. For those reasons, it feels like a direct connection to the world—unmoderated, unmitigated. Social networks are corporate middlemen by comparison. In a country that has become enchanted by local-grown food, super-economical cars, minimalist netbooks and ultra-thin televisions, Twitter is the right kind of platform: light, pure, unobtrusive, simple, elegant and endlessly accessible from any computer, mobile phone, or smart device.

Those qualities have earned it billions of dollars of free advertising as cable news, magazines and newspapers examine its societal impact. "It's awesome for Twitter, because they're getting more users," Brichter says of the publicity, "and it's awesome for me, because more people are gonna buy Tweetie. But it's also stupid." Brichter isn't fond of the direction Twitter is taking; leaving it so unsupervised has opened the door for a brand commercialism and crassness that may be sinking MySpace, and which Facebook made its reputation by avoiding. "You have a billion people screaming inane stuff," he says, "and if you've looked at the recent trends, it's all Hollywood crap. I guess it's good for me, but at the same time I didn't build Tweetie for those people," he says. "I built it for people like me."

Ironically, Brichter says he likes Twitter for one of the very reasons that Tweetie's success is never safe: its easy-come, easy-go interactivity. "I don't like Facebook or MySpace or any of those general-purpose social networks," he says. " I don't need to be 'friends' with the people I know—most of the people I know, I don't have any interest in 'what they're doing,'" he laughs. Between his two Twitter accounts—one for Tweetie and one for atebits—he follows a total of about 100 people (though he has about 10,000 followers for atebits and about 20,000 for Tweetie). Despite his commanding body of followers, he says he writes an average of "less than one" tweet everyday. "Maybe one every couple days," he estimates. "I would rather follows someone that only posted something when it was interesting." Call it economy of divulgence. Luckily for Brichter, the rest of Tweetie's user ship hasn't heard of it.

Chapter 2

Facebook

Developer Name: Joe Hewitt
Development Company: Facebook
Tags: Layout; Open Source; Client App
URL: http://facebook.com

The largest social network on earth wields tremendous power on the iPhone: its technical and visual innovations are so widely used they can become an immediate part of the iPhone UI cannon. Its task is daunting: transport Facebook's entire app platform on top of an OS that is years younger than Facebook itself (see Figure 2–1).

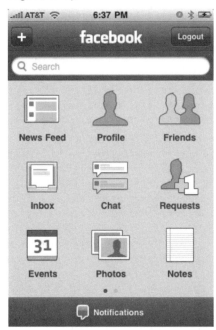

Figure 2–1. *Facebook's unique grid-like home screen, modeled after the iPhone's own.*

Joe Hewitt, who developed Facebook for iPhone, has open source roots—he worked on the Netscape on Mozilla Firefox projects—so it stands to reason that he has opened up much of his backend work to the masses. Here he discusses Facebook for iPhone's unique home screen, pictured in Figure 2–1, and its evolution from a web app to a fully-featured "phone" of its own.

As this book was going to press, Hewitt announced he would be quitting iPhone development over objections to the App Store approval process. "My decision to stop iPhone development has had everything to do with Apple's policies," he told TechCrunch.com. "I respect their right to manage their platform however they want; however I am philosophically opposed to the existence of their review process. I am very concerned that they are setting a horrible precedent for other software platforms, and soon gatekeepers will start infesting the lives of every software developer." He will remain at Facebook pursuing other projects.[1]

How did you become the sole iPhone developer at Facebook?

When I started at Facebook, I built iphone.facebook.com, which is now touch.facebook.com (Figure 2–2). After that, I asked to do an iPhone app. Pretty much my whole two years at Facebook has been doing iPhone things.

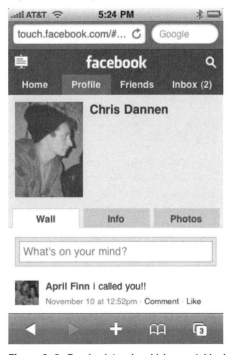

Figure 2–2. *Facebook touch, which uses tabbed navigation.*

---

[1] http://www.techcrunch.com/2009/11/11/joe-hewitt-developer-of-facebooks-massively-popular-iphone-app-quits-the-project/

Yet Facebook Touch looks much different than the iPhone app.

The touch web site is now geared, not only for iPhone, but Android, Palm, and so on, so we're limited in how much we want to make it modeled after the iPhone conventions. I think the two will diverge more, if anything; other people are working on the touch web site now. They might take it in a slightly different direction.

Why isn't a static nav bar at the bottom of the screen useful for Facebook?

The first version of the app did have the tab bar at the bottom, but I took it out because I feel like Facebook is a platform in itself, and each of the tabs were almost like apps in and of themselves that really called for use of the full screen.

I had to look forward; we have a lot of new apps coming down the pipe, and I felt like the model Facebook works on lends itself better to sort of being a "phone" in and of itself. Facebook has its own chat, phone book, mail, photos, and applications, so squeezing it all into tabs made it feel too limited. Going with this model—it's a home screen just like the iPhone home screen—will let it grow and become full-featured. It also gives us room to add more apps within our app.

What was the thinking behind the grid interface?

I haven't really seen other apps that do this, and I wouldn't really recommend that anyone else do it. Facebook is kind of unique in its breadth and the amount of stuff people do on it. I really hesitated to build in the grid for a while, but as I kept moving things around and trying to make it all fit into the tab bar, I just felt like this was the best solution. I was expecting more people to complain about it, but it seems to have worked out pretty well.

You also use the top nav in an interesting way in this new version. Is the redesign a consequence of implementing the grid?

The grid came first; the feed filters you're referring to were, in the previous version, in a horizontally-scrolling tab-bar at the top. It just didn't seem that people were using it enough to justify having a full-time piece of screen allocated to it, so I thought the new design was just more appropriate for how infrequently [feeds are] used. (Figure 2–3 shows the Facebook feed filter, which uses Apple's rolling dial selector.)

Figure 2–3. *Facebook's feed filter. "The new design was just more appropriate for how infrequently [feeds are] used," says Hewitt.*

What are the compromises involved in using the grid?

Economy [of taps] is always a motivating factor, but the grid adds an extra tap [because you need to press the grid button] versus the full-time tab bar. That was a compromise I felt was necessary. There's always that balance between screen clutter—adding tabs— and the number of taps.

What went into creating Facebook's view controllers?

I did a lot of custom stuff. The app is built on an open source framework I created called Three20, and it uses its own view controllers, all of which I had to write. I had to try to reinvent the Apple photo browsing app and the Apple Mail composing tool, among other stuff.

Three20 also has a style system meant to emulate CSS. If you want to draw any graphics, Apple normally requires you to use Quartz and these heavy-handed frameworks. And I wanted a simpler way of doing that, so I created one in Three20 and a lot of people have picked it up and added things to it for their own purposes.

Another custom thing is in the friends list (shown in Figure 2–4). When I first started working on the app, I thought it would be cool to have phone numbers be really handy. The first two versions didn't really convey that information well; you could get the numbers by clicking on a profile and clicking over to the info tab, but I thought it'd be better to surface the numbers in an icon in the list.

Figure 2–4. *Facebook shows which of your friends have listed phone numbers on their profile pages, and allows you to call them with one click.*

Is it tempting to start playing with MapKit and add friend-mapping?

Yes, definitely. I don't have much I can talk about there, but it's definitely something we think about a lot. I wouldn't be surprised if that's in Facebook in the future.

Is there a point where the Facebook app gets too big?

On the 3GS, I don't feel like I'm pushing that limit yet, but the previous devices were sluggish for sure. The 3GS gives us a lot of room to grow. When you're looking at photos on the 3G, we definitely see a lot more out-of-memory crashes [than on the 3GS.] The JPEGs that you download are not exactly scaled to the screen of the iPhone, so you're downloading images that are a little bigger than they need to be—so holding them in memory and juggling them can cause the device to freak out sometimes. I've spent a lot time optimizing.

When the app gets memory warnings from the OS, how does it deal with them?

Well, there's a lot of data that's cached. For instance, when you load the news feed, you're getting each individual update, but also the names and pictures of the user that posted the update. We cache all that so you don't have to keep loading that if you go to another part of the app (Figure 2–5 shows Facebook's events page). That way if you go to view a message from someone who have in memory from a news feed update, their information is already there. If there's a low memory warning then all that stuff gets flushed and has to be downloaded again.

Figure 2–5. *Facebook caches old news and events. "It feels nicer to see something right away that you can interact with," says Hewitt.*

Otherwise, it all stays cached?

Everything in the app works that way. There's a disk cache so if you load events, notes, or requests, it's cached so when you go back to the app, and we show the cached version. And as we show it, we try to load the latest version. If it's a week old—or some number of days, I forget the exact number—the app will just show you "loading" and clear the old stuff.

Before that system was in place, you were constantly looking at a little spinner wherever you went —loading, loading, loading. I think it feels nicer to see something right away that you can interact with while the new stuff is coming in.

We actually didn't even have events until this third version. That kind of stuff definitely could be surfaced in a lot of other places, which would also feel nice. I've been thinking about putting your upcoming events on the top of news feed, so you don't have to go to the Events app.

Listing 2–1 is an excerpt of the Three20 framework. It illustrates that composing a POST response to a Web server can involve a lot of work -- and how Three20 takes care of all that verbosity for you.

Listing 2–1. *The Facebook App's Disk Cache Framework (Snippet)*

```
(NSData*)generatePostBody {
NSMutableData *body = [NSMutableData data];
NSString *beginLine = [NSString stringWithFormat:@"\r\n--%@\r\n", kStringBoundary];

  [body appendData:[[NSString stringWithFormat:@"--%@\r\n", kStringBoundary]
    dataUsingEncoding:NSUTF8StringEncoding]];

  for (id key in [_parameters keyEnumerator]) {
    NSString* value = [_parameters valueForKey:key];
    if (![value isKindOfClass:[UIImage class]]) {
      [body appendData:[beginLine dataUsingEncoding:NSUTF8StringEncoding]];
      [body appendData:[[NSString
        stringWithFormat:@"Content-Disposition: form-data; name=\"%@\"\r\n\r\n", key]
          dataUsingEncoding:NSUTF8StringEncoding]];
      [body appendData:[value dataUsingEncoding:NSUTF8StringEncoding]];
    }
  }

  NSString* imageKey = nil;
  for (id key in [_parameters keyEnumerator]) {
    if ([[_parameters objectForKey:key] isKindOfClass:[UIImage class]]) {
      UIImage* image = [_parameters objectForKey:key];
      CGFloat quality = [TTURLRequestQueue mainQueue].imageCompressionQuality;
      NSData* data = UIImageJPEGRepresentation(image, quality);

      [body appendData:[beginLine dataUsingEncoding:NSUTF8StringEncoding]];
      [body appendData:[[NSString stringWithFormat:
                  @"Content-Disposition: form-data; name=\"%@\";
filename=\"image.jpg\"\r\n",
                  key]
          dataUsingEncoding:NSUTF8StringEncoding]];
      [body appendData:[[NSString
        stringWithFormat:@"Content-Length: %d\r\n", data.length]
          dataUsingEncoding:NSUTF8StringEncoding]];
      [body appendData:[[NSString
        stringWithString:@"Content-Type: image/jpeg\r\n\r\n"]
          dataUsingEncoding:NSUTF8StringEncoding]];
      [body appendData:data];
      imageKey = key;
    }
  }

  for (NSInteger i = 0; i < _files.count; i += 3) {
    NSData* data = [_files objectAtIndex:i];
    NSString* mimeType = [_files objectAtIndex:i+1];
    NSString* fileName = [_files objectAtIndex:i+2];

    [body appendData:[beginLine dataUsingEncoding:NSUTF8StringEncoding]];
    [body appendData:[[NSString stringWithFormat:
                  @"Content-Disposition: form-data; name=\"%@\";
filename=\"%@\"\r\n",
```

```
                              fileName, fileName]
                dataUsingEncoding:NSUTF8StringEncoding]];
        [body appendData:[[NSString stringWithFormat:@"Content-Length: %d\r\n", data.length]
                dataUsingEncoding:NSUTF8StringEncoding]];
        [body appendData:[[NSString stringWithFormat:@"Content-Type: %@\r\n\r\n", mimeType]
                dataUsingEncoding:NSUTF8StringEncoding]];
        [body appendData:data];
    }

    [body appendData:[[NSString stringWithFormat:@"\r\n--%@--\r\n", kStringBoundary]
                    dataUsingEncoding:NSUTF8StringEncoding]];

    // If an image was found, remove it from the dictionary to save memory while we
    // perform the upload
    if (imageKey) {
      [_parameters removeObjectForKey:imageKey];
    }

    //TTLOG  (@"Sending %s", [body bytes]);
    return body;
}

//////////////////////////////////////////////////////////////////////////////////////
//////////
```

Why couldn't Facebook for iPhone have kept growing in its old layout?

Well, tabs are very effective as long as you only have one level of tabs. A lot of apps—including the previous Facebook app—have two levels of tabs, which I think becomes troubling. I see that a lot, that people are trying to cram a lot onto this little screen, and that second row of tabs becomes tempting when you have two levels of hierarchy to navigate. But having one level of tabs is a great way to navigate.

But how different can you make your UI without alienating people?

That's a big question. I hear it both ways and I do emulate Apple quite a bit. Our message inbox is a lot like Mail. But where I feel like it doesn't fit, I just do things a little differently. I'm not crazy about the way they do push notifications. Once you get more than one app sending you notifications, including SMS, it becomes very awkward. I have a Palm Pre to play around with, and the way they handle notifications is just perfect. Any app can send something to that little bar on the bottom, and they all balance really well; the card spec is also really great. I think that apple has a lot of work to do. We're working on push notifications for our app now [for messages, but not chat], but if it worked the way it does on the Pre, I'd be a lot happier. On the iPhone, you actually have to hit OK to dismiss it, which sucks. On the Pre you're not forced to attend to it at all.

As the app grows, how will you handle preferences?

Our app does use the Settings app for preferences right now, but we only have three toggles and they're not that important. We're going to have a few more, and I've been planning to switch over to putting all our settings inside the app. Otherwise people just don't find them.

What's going to be most enticing about future versions of the Facebook app?

I think exploring the idea of sharing your location is very exciting. It's a huge untapped opportunity, and a challenging one for us. It's so obvious. People are like, why haven't you done it yet? But it's a really difficult thing to get right, and can easily be semi-useless if not done carefully. We could build the technical stuff very easily, but it's tougher to make it so that people actually want to use it, and would habitually use it. There are a ton of services out there that do that right now, but how many have really picked up steam? Foursquare tries to make a game out of it to motivate people that way, but I'm not sure we want to make a game out of it. I think part of it is just people's expectations; if everyone decided to use it, they would start to expect to be able to go on Facebook to find out where their friends are. You wouldn't have to update your status to say, "I'm at the bar," because it would just implicitly include that information. If we can ever get there, to have people using it by default, then it'll be useful. But getting people to do it when no one else is doing it isn't easy.

How do you incentivize people to start caring about a feature?

I don't think we have a good answer for that yet.

Are the mobile versions of Facebook diverging from desktop Facebook?

When I was building this app, I was always kind of thinking that someday people will use [Facebook] more from their mobile devices than from their computers. So much of what goes into Facebook is useful to you when you're out and about—a lot of status updates are mobile, and things like calendar events obviously are very useful, and photo uploads, too. The percentage of our traffic that goes through mobile is incredible, and growing rapidly.

If anything's going to change, it's that Facebook mobile will become the most frequently used version of Facebook, and the desktop version will only be used for certain tasks—writing long messages or uploading a ton of photos. But as we see our traffic numbers swinging toward mobile, it changes how we decide what features to add and what to promote. There's been some features that started on the mobile side and came over [to the Web], and definitely the iPhone app has started to be the model for all our mobile apps and web sites.

Are there interesting ways you use Apple's frameworks?

I think I've actually under-used Apple's frameworks. There's a lot of really cool stuff in there that I haven't found a good use for—like Core Location, OpenGL, and MapKit. But at the same time, I've found Apple's actual tools to be under-serving my needs. I had to write my own photo-browser and my own message-composer, which was a huge effort.

It would be nice if they could include something so commonly needed. They have a framework for picking a photo from your collection, but only from the albums on the phone—you can't insert your own photos into that UI. It's a very generic thing. A lot of apps use that finger-flicking display of images. That's the most popular part of the Three20 framework. I would not be surprised if a future iPhone OS has that baked in.

Are there any interesting ways your Three20 frameworks have been used by the open source community?

I know the Flickr app uses it, and there are quite a few others. I developed it under my name; there's no dedicated site for it, but it's hosted on GitHub. The Facebook app was just so big that I ended up writing a lot of code that was worth sharing, so I thought it would be useful to open-source it.

Why did you choose to make Three20 open source?

I'm an employee of Facebook, so I'm not out there trying to make money on the market. It was work I was being paid to do, and Facebook has a good policy toward open source—they try to let their engineers open source anything that's not too uniquely valuable to the company. I've had a history of doing open source before, with Mozilla, so I try to make things open whenever I can. People do appreciate that, and it makes me feel good that my work is affecting more than one app on the store.

Part II

Using App Connectivity with Core Location to Make Games Social

The iPhone is fun, from code on up. Screens flip, slide, and spin when they change state. App-buttons jiggle. Everything about it seems to insinuate light-heartedness. Even basic navigation feels like finger-painting.

But fun on the iPhone has an interesting duality to it. There's the self-contained kind of fun that comes from gaming: graphically rich, challenging, time-wasting, brain-bending, and solitary. With the headphones in your ears, games help you relax into a world of your own.

But iPhone-fun can also be completely extroverted: iPhone as social lubricant. It lets you mass-text, conference call, IM, Skype, and share location, so that you can better integrate your world with others'.

Topple 2 and Foursquare come from opposing corners, but they share a reliance on connectivity. Topple's engineers use analytics from the game to adjust level difficulty on the fly, and have built a massive networking initiative Ngmoco calls "Plus+," all meant to keep you coming back into the Ngmoco world when you find yourself in a "free cycle."

Foursquare's connectivity is meant to catapult you into the real world: bars, restaurants, and clubs. The app is all about geolocating you and your friends, of course, but there's more than just that. The Foursquare team used WebView to keep their app design dynamic, allowing them to roll it out quickly and perform updates on the server side.

In their own ways, both apps create nearly Pavlovian responses in users looking for something to do. That's the difference between amusing apps and truly addictive ones.

Chapter 3

Topple 2

Developer Name: Bob Stevenson and Allen Ma
Development Company: Ngmoco:)
Tags: Release Strategy; Fun; Connectivity; Art
URL: `http://ngmoco.com`

"On the iPhone, it's really about being respectful of peoples' time," says Ngmoco Founder and Chief Creative Officer Bob Stevenson. An odd mantra for a company that makes video games, the ultimate diversion—and surprisingly sober for a bunch of guys who measure their analytics in "awesomes." Figure 3–1 shows the home screen of Ngmoco's Topple 2.

Figure 3–1. *Topple's home screen.*

The "awesome" could be called the standard measurement of the Ngmoco realm, and it comes from one of the company's first games, Mazefinger. Mazefinger and Topple 1 were twins, released at the same time in October 2008. "Every time a player completes a maze, the word "awesome" comes out," says Stevenson. "So we have an analytic that tells us we've had half a billion awesomes." That, in a nutshell, is Ngmoco: precision silliness, the kind of fun that is amusing to 13–year-old iPod touch owners and 35-year-old iPhoners alike. And it's that just that quality that has pushed four of their games into App Store's top-five gaming list, and that won Topple 2 its ADA. What is the weird science of engineering fun? And why does it involve so much respect?

How to Do a Sequel: Conceptually

Allen Ma, the associate at Ngmoco who managed Topple 2, says that his team tried to stick to an age-old game-developer rule of thumb, brought to the company by Ngmoco's other founder, Neil Young. Young, who was previously the general manager of Electronic Arts' Los Angeles office, brought with him the rule of thirds: "When you're doing a sequel," Ma says, "one third is new, one third is improved, and one third is the same." The goal, he says, is altering just the right amount of the game experience. "It's about adding enough to the game to make it different, but yet still keep the overall feel, so that the existing player-base will still appreciate the game," Ma says. But that requires parsing a game into discrete parts, and asking a lot of nebulous questions. What exactly makes the game "feel" the way it does? What's boring? What's outdated? What's the most fun?

Ma says that Ngmoco believed they knew what had made Topple 1 a success, and the team used it as a diving rod for the rest of Topple 2's features. "We wanted to keep it a short, immersive experience," he says. That immersive experience is part of what brought the Apple Design judges to their decision: all told, Topple 2 makes use of UIKit, OpenGL ES, Bonjour, CFNetwork, email, Twitter, and Facebook, to say nothing of the accelerometer and multi-touch. "We fully engage you with the device; it really does feel like you're stacking blocks," says Ma.

But that immersion is what requires so much respect for players' time, says Stevenson, who moved to California after growing up outside Edinburgh, Scotland, to make games. "You need to be making games as services. People need to be able to pop in and pop out of your game fast," he says. The less cognitive load for the player, the more likely your game will end up the go-to game out of dozens of others on the player's phone. "It means more quality and more intensity," Stevenson says. As of this writing, Ngmoco is in the midst of developing a first-person shooter game that allows players to battle opponents over a 3G connection. Stevenson says his team has designed the game to revolve around hyperactive three-minute sessions of play, because anything longer probably isn't realistic on an iPhone OS device. Ma has a more technical definition of the concept. "We talk about peoples' time in terms of 'free cycles.' So you're using your device for all these other things, but then every once and a while, you have this free cycle," he says. "So we want to create a game where someone enjoys it and can play it really quickly, so when they do have a free cycle, our game is on the top of their mind." The free-cycle approach has led Ngmoco to design its games with a three-minute window of playability in mind; if gamers can't get some kind of satisfaction in within three minutes, they might lose out to another game the next time a user gets a free cycle. "We want you to fill that time with Topple 2," Ma says.

In Topple 1, the "feeling" of stacking blocks was enough to gin up players' enthusiasm, but Topple 2 needed more. "With Topple 2, we sort of tried to create more of a universe around the game, because before, in Topple 1, there was just sort of an interface," Ma says. They did that by adding a narrative structure: who were these perverse-looking blocks, and what else could they do? "We wanted to make you feel like you were progressing through a world, this Topple World, where there are all these different zones, and all these Topple blocks behave in different ways," Ma says. Topple 1 was immersion in a physical experience: touching the blocks, watching them list from side to side. Topple 2 became more of a mental immersion, with several new modes of play. "We had a core game experience that was basically stacking blocks upward," Ma says, "and we were trying to add to that by creating games that you'd do in real life. You don't just stack things straight up in real life. You build things."

And when you build things, you make progress. While it's good to be a fast, convenient game-as-service, ultimately the real fun derives from beating whatever challenge is presented, and moving forward into new territory. Without the promise of progress, there's not the compulsion to go back into the game again and again. "We discussed how Topple 1 didn't feel like there was any progression, since the [level] interface was just a bunch of level buttons that unlocked," says Ma. At meetings, Ma brought up iconic games like World of Goo and Super Mario Brothers 3, which had guides to players' progress in the form of otherworldly maps. "We thought that style of map would convey a lot," he says. Stevenson worked with Ghostbot, a San Francisco art and graphics house with plenty of games and feature animated films to their credit. Ma says Stevenson "sketched out the idea in his head," deciding that he wanted a map that rose upward as new levels were unlocked. Ghostbot came up with the world pictured in Figure 3–2.

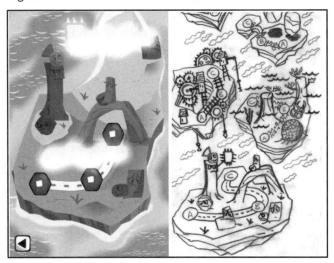

Figure 3–2. *Stevenson worked with Ghostbot to produce the first sketches for the Topple 2 world.*

The push for a Topple universe also led to new modes of play. In Rescue Mode, pictured in Figure 3–4, an egg drops from the top of the screen onto your stack of blocks, which you have to rearrange to slowly bring the egg down to the ground without breaking. Another mode, Balancer, presents you with a lever-like scale that only awards points when perfectly balanced. Questioning the orientation of gameplay also led to rethinking the physical behavior of the blocks: the blocks feel heavy in regular gameplay, but what if they were made of Styrofoam and meant to float? Experimentation led to the underwater level, an early mockup of which is seen in Figure 3–3. This level, Ma says, "fit very well with our anti-gravity idea, as it was easy to relay to the users that the blocks were lighter than water and wanted to float to the surface."

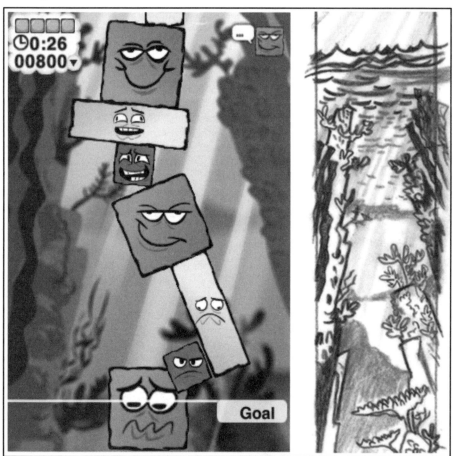

Figure 3–3. *The sketch for the underwater level, right, and the final product.*

New ways to play with blocks might seem like superficial add-ons at first, but they did something else: they brought Topple even deeper into the iPhone's philosophical fold. Nearly symmetrical from top to bottom and left to right, both iPod Touch and iPhone were meant to be devices with flexible and fungible orientations. Once the Topple team unlocked that same flexibility in the game, gameplay became vastly more creative.

How to Do a Sequel: Technically

Topple 1 was a great game; Topple 2 is a better one. Sounds simple, but it takes a lot of technical grafts to make it happen. "The design challenge for trying to refresh and enhance a game you've previously made is very different from coming up with a complete unique idea," says Stevenson, who has a background in art and design and began designing games for the Commodore 64. That's especially true if your codebase wasn't built to be modular and which was already pushing the limits of the iPhone's memory, as with Topple.

Figure 3–4. *Topple's rescue mode requires you to use blocks to keep a golden egg from breaking.*

At first, Topple 2 was going to be an incremental improvement: a few new levels, and new menus. "We were working off the codebase of a single player game," says Ryan Evans, vice president of Muteki Corporation, which Ngmoco hired to develop Topple 2, and one of two coders that worked on the project. "The original design specs called for some updates to a single player game, and then the multiplayer [idea] comes along," says Evans, who is based in Emeryville, CA. "And then challenge mode comes along. And then, well, you get the idea." Evans and the other Muteki engineer, Jason Young, threw hundreds of hours at the project. "It was a real bear to wrangle some of those features in to code that simply wasn't designed for it," he says.

One of those features: Challenge Mode, which allows players to throw down the gauntlet with a friend by sending them a challenge via Facebook or Twitter. Connectivity was one of the features that won Topple 2 its ADA, so it's worth taking a look at how the app interacts with the two services. Here's how Topple issues its challenges.

It uses one of the iPhone's most ingenious sharing conduits: the ability for an app to send information, even when offline, by generating an URL and sending it in Mail.

"It's a pretty useful hack, and is a great way to get challenge functionality working on social platforms like Twitter that don't really offer much in the way of attaching additional information to a post," says Evans. "I also think it's a great method for smaller shops who can't necessarily afford a full infrastructure."

The data-URL functions in several ways for Topple 2. Firstly, it allows players to send and receive challenges even when they weren't around a cellular or WiFi connection; if a player issues a challenge while, say, on a subway, it simply gets stored in the Mail outbox until it can be delivered. During development, it also kept Topple 2's engineers from having to dedicate a server to mediating challenges, or from having to build establish an interface with Apple's servers to deliver Push notifications. (Figure 3–5: Twitter challenges in a public stream.)

"Challenge data" in the URL, refers to a series of block-height samples taken during a player's "free play" mode, which denotes simple block stacking.

Per Apple's instructions, the formulae for Topple's URLs look like this:

```
topple2://<base 64 encoded challenge data>:<base 64 encoded challenge info block>
```

"Interpolating between these gave a nice smooth 'ghost' that felt snappy and alive," says Evans.

The "challenge info" block was a later addition, he says, and includes information about the challenger (their Twitter or Facebook name, for example) as well as the vector through which the player received the challenge. "That let us be a bit more intelligent with the 're-challenge' functionality, automatically defaulting the re-challenge to the posting method of the original challenge," Evans says.

Figure 3–5. *Twitter challenges appear in a public timeline inside Topple 2.*

Generating the data-URL could be done as illustrated in this sample project:

```objc
- (NSURL *)URLWithParameters:(NSDictionary *)parameters
{
  BOOL isFirstParam = YES;
  NSMutableString *urlString =
  [NSMutableString stringWithString:@"yourgamescheme://domain.com/"];

  for (id key in parameters)
  {
    NSString *value = [parameters objectForKey:key];
    [urlString appendFormat:@"%@%@=%@", (isFirstParam ? @"?" : @"&"), key, value];
    isFirstParam = NO;
  }
  return [NSURL URLWithString:
  [urlString stringByAddingPercentEscapesUsingEncoding:NSUTF8StringEncoding]];
}

// Build a dictionary with named parameters
NSDictionary *parameters = [NSDictionary dictionaryWithObjectsAndKeys:
@"Garry Kasparov", @"challenger",
```

```
[NSDate date], @"date",
[NSNumber numberWithInt:1], @"opponent-color", nil];

NSLog (@"url = %@", [self URLWithParameters:parameters]);
```

The log statement prints out:
url = yourgamescheme://domain.com/?challenger=Garry%20Kasparov&opponent-
color=1&date=2009-10-02%2014:22:46%20+0200

Disseminating a challenge is one thing, but there's a lot more at work behind Topple 2's challenges. The app interfaces with Twitter and Facebook to allow players to hit up friends and followers for gameplay. Here's how it checks for challenges issues, and acts on them.

```
//
//  FacebookTwitterDemoAppDelegate.m
//  FacebookTwitterDemo
//
//  Created by Ryan Evans on 9/1/09.
//  Copyright Muteki Corporation 2009. All rights reserved.
//

#import "FacebookTwitterDemoAppDelegate.h"
#import "FacebookTwitterDemoViewController.h"

@implementation FacebookTwitterDemoAppDelegate

@synthesize window;
@synthesize viewController;

- (BOOL)application:(UIApplication *)application
didFinishLaunchingWithOptions:(NSDictionary *)launchOptions {

    // Override point for customization after app launch
    [window addSubview:viewController.view];
    [window makeKeyAndVisible];
            NGChallengeStrings* strings = [[NGChallengeStrings alloc] init];
            strings.twitterSearch =
@"http://search.twitter.com/search.json?q=%23FacebookTwitterDemo+tinyurl.com&rpp=10";
            strings.tinyURLFormat = @"http://tinyurl.com/api-create.php?url=%@";
            strings.eMailMsg = @"This is a message for a challenge, you should click
here: %@";
            strings.eMailRechallengeMsg = @"This is a message for a re-challenge, you
should click here: %@";
            strings.eMailRechallengeSubj = @"FacebookTwitterDemo Rechallenge!";
            strings.eMailSubj = @"FacebookTwitterDemo Challenge!";
            strings.facebookPost = @"Can you beat my FacebookTwitterDemo challenge?
Click here: %@";
            strings.facebookRechallenge = @"I smoked your FacebookTwitterDemo
challenge, can you beat mine? %@";
            strings.gameURLFormat = @"facebooktwitterdemo://a/?q=%s";
            strings.urlHeader = @"facebooktwitterdemo://a/?q=";

            [NGChallengeSystem getInstance].localizedStrings = strings;
            [NGChallengeSystem getInstance].window = window;
            [NGChallengeSystem getInstance].delegate = self;
               [strings release];
```

```
                // If this statement is omitted, memory will leak.

                if([launchOptions objectForKey:UIApplicationLaunchOptionsURLKey] != nil) {
                        NSURL* toHandle = [launchOptions
objectForKey:UIApplicationLaunchOptionsURLKey];
                        NSLog(@"Opened with URL, need to parse it!");
                        [[NGChallengeSystem getInstance] parseChallengeURL:[toHandle
absoluteString]];
                        return YES;
                }

                return NO;
}

- (void)dealloc {
    [viewController release];
    [window release];
    [super dealloc];
}


- (void)receivedTwitterChallengeFromUser:(NSString*)user withData:(NSData*)data {
        // In this method you would do something with the challenge data to load up your
challenge and play it.
        // For now we just create a string and print it out to validate the data
was accurate
        NSString* string = [[NSString alloc] initWithData:data
encoding:NSUTF8StringEncoding];
        NSLog(@"Got a twitter challenge with string contents %@ from player: %@",
string, user);
        [string release];
}
        // If this statement is omitted, memory will leak.

- (void)receivedFacebookChallengeFromUser:(NSString*)user withData:(NSData*)data
andFBUID:(FBUID)challengerUID {
        // In this method you would do something with the challenge data to load up
your challenge and play it.
        // For now we just create a string and print it out to validate the data
was accurate
        NSString* string = [[NSString alloc] initWithData:data
encoding:NSUTF8StringEncoding];
        NSLog(@"Got a twitter challenge with string contents %@ from uid %lld |
player: %@", string, challengerUID, user);
        [string release];
}
        // If this statement is omitted, memory will leak.

@end
```

Designing Apps (and Companies) for the Mass Market

The data-URL hack also had another benefit for Topple 2 players: it allowed challenge mode to be just as effectual on an iPod Touch as on the iPhone. "It hadn't occurred to us how influential the iPod Touch was going to be," says Stevenson. "It effectively doubled the market." When Topple 1 entered the App Store in October of 2008, the iPhone was its natural milieu—but when Topple 2 entered the App Store five months later there were tens of millions of iPhone OS devices sold and almost half of them iPods. That created some complications: for Topple 2, they'd have to add features and functionality, and yet appeal to a lower common denominator. "You have to design for the iPod Touch upwards," Stevenson says.

But 70 million users presents another design quandary: deciding on a target audience. "Who is the market? The market is everyone," Stevenson says. "The next question becomes: who do you focus on? It can be tricky, depending on the game," he adds. "Our stance is that our marketing is aimed at ages 12 to 19," he says, "and to adults that feel like they're 12 to 19."

Though Stevenson says he didn't think much about his market in 2008, Topple's trademark block-faces were drawn with both kids and adults in mind. "I thought, let's try and make this look a little bit nicer than people would expect on a phone," he says. "Rather than just blocks, is there a way to give them personality?" For art, Stevenson approached Ghostbot. "They weren't sure what kind of company we were, so at first they drew really friendly unthreatening faces that were almost like kids' cartoons," he says. "So I drew one sort of face with a malevolent smile which ended up being the face of the game. It's not meant to be dark, but I said, 'What if this family of blocks was dysfunctional? I thought, there's going to be a lot of adults playing this. Kids will just find it cool that there are faces, but for adults you want something else. You don't want it to feel like Dante's Inferno, but the notion that they look like they have a tiny bit of personality I don't think ended up hurting the look of the game." In short, he says, the key is personality with unspecific appeal. "It's about great design, plus a mass market idea. That's the kind of design that we're trying to create."

The market may yet grow. With persistent rumors swirling of an Apple tablet running a modified iPhone OS, Apple's handheld following may expand even further to include enterprise, small business, and digital arts customers. Finding a way to pull them in for a short, immersive experience—and having a code-base ready for modification—may make mass-market even more important among an ever-growing field of competitors.

"The size of the market is great, but the amount of product in the market can make it really difficult to have a healthy ecosystem where people can find each other's products, Stevenson says. "We guessed that would be the case, that's why we set ourselves up as a game publisher rather than a developer." Though Ngmoco employs a staff of around 15, it farms actual development out to contractors around the world. Stevenson says he anticipated that with Apple offering 70 cents on the dollar for apps, the best developers might not concede to working in-house when they could go get rich on their own. The way Apple has it set up, everyone should do it, and everyone did do it," Stevenson says. Instead of hiring on a big staff, Ngmoco relies on talented, self-sufficient coders. "These guys can really do it all themselves—maybe they need some art, but they're really into design and really into programming. They tend to do it as a lifestyle, they're not in it for the money, so they're strongly opinionated, but really good design shops," he says.

Sourcing engineering also keeps stress levels low for everyone involved. Stevenson calls in-house development a "a quite draining type of activity." "You tend to become one big dysfunctional family," he says. "The entire organization becomes defined by the endeavor they're working on. We thought, we'll come up with ideas, but we'll also listen to really good ideas, or buy projects, or contract teams so that they're autonomous."

Another facet of the lean-company strategy is super-fast development. He chose independent game developer Chris DeLeon for Topple 1, who he says was perfect for the project, and set a project timeline of eight weeks. "At the end of game Chris said, 'I'll never do an eight-week project again, it's just too long,'" says Stevenson. "That's funny coming from my traditional experience—the longest game I ever worked on was three years. And this young guy in his mid-twenties was like, 'I can't believe you took me on this death march of eight weeks.'" By moving fast and using independent, self-sufficient talent, Ngmoco may have avoided much of the infighting and friction that is anathema to building something fun. "It was a simple, powerful idea: let's make this quick, let's make it successful, and let's make it fun," says Stevenson.

Managing a Universe

"We had a lot of memory issues with Topple 2 throughout the course of development," says Evans. Some, he says, were inherited from Topple 1, but others got bigger as the list of changes grew. One problem: not having a comprehensive caching system in place for textures.

A good example of this, according to Evans: "The original code was using [UIImage imageNamed:] to load the UIImage* objects for a texture. It's a nice call, because it's very simple to use, but the flipside is that imageNamed creates its own cache of images in memory." That was causing the phone to keep lots of extra copies of image data wasting memory while that method was still being used. "When we switched to one of the alternate image loading methods, our memory usage dropped dramatically," he says.

PVRTC-It

Another texture issue that the team didn't get to resolve: the use of PNG files. "Everything I've seen says that PVRTC will give you loads more memory to work with, since you can pass the images compressed directly to OpenGL ES," Evans says, "but we were never able to get the Topple 2 assets sufficiently good looking in PVRTC to make the jump over." He says that future games, whether Topple offspring or otherwise, will make use of the PVRTC format.

Stevenson's mantra of respect for the user extends to memory management as well. "The iPhone seems to be pretty good at writing small blocks of data quickly, so we tried to keep the overall size of the save data low," Evans says. "Partially this is out of respect to the user and not taking up a gigantic amount of space on their device, and partially because the less data there is, the faster saving and loading can go."

While Topple 2 didn't make use of PVRTC, more memory-hungry apps might necessitate it—especially on 2G and 3G iPhones without benefit of the 256MB of RAM in the 3GS. So what is it? PVRTC (or PowerVR Texture Compression) is a format you can use to compress textures and save memory during expensive operations. OpenGL ES 2.0 supports the format by implementing an extension called GL_IMG_texture_compression_pvrtc. There are two levels of PVRTC compression: 4 and 2 bits per channel, which respectively offer a 8:1 and 16:1 compression ratio over the uncompressed (32-bit) texture. Image quality is a legitimate concern, especially in apps like Topple 2, which pride themselves on art. But for most applications, the 3–bit compression level still allows for decent-looking results, and apps that make heavy use of PVRTC compression (like AccuTerra, also profiled in this book) are living proof. Apple claims that using this format frequently saves more memory than reducing image size.

The iPhone SDK includes a tool called Texturetool that allows you to convert PNGs into this special compression format. Texturetool gives you flexibility to find a balance between image quality and size. The tool is located at the directory /Developer/Platforms/iPhoneOS.platform/Developer/usr/bin/texturetool (provided the iPhone SDK is installed in the default location.)

As always, a downside of using special file formats is the potential for obsolescence. Because future iPhones and iPods might not use the Imagination Technologies's PowerVR MBX SDK for OpenGL ES processing, take care to preserve all textures somewhere in the app as uncompressed PNGs, so that future devices can still load the images even without PVRTC support. To ensure that the app doesn't end up floundering on some future iPhone because of this issue, be sure to include the following simple boolean expression in its code to check for the proper OpenGL extensions for PVRTC.

```
BOOL CheckForExtension(NSString *searchName)
{
// For best results, extensionsNames should be stored in your renderer so that it does not
// need to be recreated on each invocation.
    NSString *extensionsString = [NSString stringWithCString:glGetString(GL_EXTENSIONS)
encoding: NSASCIIStringEncoding];
    NSArray *extensionsNames = [extensionsString componentsSeparatedByString:@" "];
    return [extensionsNames containsObject: searchName];
}
```

If an app is unable to use compressed images, there are other best practices for speeding through OpenGL ES. Some options: use lower-precision color formats like RGB565, RGBA5551, or RGBA4444. Also ensure that the app is using appropriately small dimensions in its images, is loading them at initialization and not during runtime, and that it avoids changing OpenGL ES state as much as possible.

To achieve the latter, try combining smaller textures into a single "texture atlas," which the system can pick from to find certain textures within the atlas. As Apple's documentation states: "A texture atlas allows multiple models to be drawn without changing the bound texture and may also allow multiple glDrawElements calls to be collapsed into a single call."

Using mimaps for all appropriate textures can also cut down on the number of texels being fetched from texture memory, which saves on memory bandwidth. The GL_LINEAR_MIPMAP_LINEAR filter mode provide the best quality when texturing, but is less miserly than the GL_LINEAR_MIPMAP_NEAREST filter mode instead, which will spare even more bandwidth but may cause quality to suffer.

In keeping with minimizing state-changes, it might also be a good idea to instruct an app to perform multiple steps of an algorithm on each pass of the app's geometry. Called "multitexturing," the practice involves calling both of OpenGL ES's available texture units with the call glGetIntegerv with GL_MAX_TEXTURE_UNITS as the parameter.

Fun, the Apple Way

Though Stevenson and his team have decades of gaming experience between them—as artists, developers, and enthusiasts—most of it was on at-home consoles like the PC or Xbox. "The mobile game business before the iPhone was something that would never have interested us at all," he says. At the time the Apple device was announced, Stevenson was CEO and co-founder at Project Moon Studios in San Francisco, where he oversaw successful titles like Smartypants for the Nintendo Wii and Citizen Kabuto for the PC. "Having worked on practically ever single console ever created I was intrigued to see how powerful the phone would be," he says. "No one had any idea until someone build the first game, and then we realized: oh, we can really make games on this."

At the time, his future co-founder, Neil Young, was managing the LA branch of mega-gamemaker EA. Young approached Stevenson and suggested they think about what kind of company could be built around the iPhone. "By the time we finished our business plan, I flew back to spend time with my dad, who is an old-school businessman and doesn't really suffer any bad ideas," Stevenson says. "And we kicked ideas around for what we thought this business would be, and we came to the conclusion that we thought this would be a revolution."

Why? "Because it was the answer to a lot of things that we saw on the horizon and beforehand," he says. "We were really interested in the notion that the computer was moving towards people instead of people moving towards the computer. And we thought that would fundamentally change the way they spend their time, and therefore how they played games. So before the game aspect of the phone was unlocked, we knew the phone had an accelerometer, so you could move the device and control it, and we knew it was connected—it has all your friends, all your mail, it's a personal device. And it's a phone. It's got a microphone and a camera built in," says Stevenson, who has also developed for Sony's PSP. "You also have what is essentially four finger touch—all those things combined make you realize that it's an interesting palette to work with."

Before departing Project Moon to start Ngmoco, which is backed by the joint-venture Apple/Kleiner Perkins iFund, Stevenson was fresh of the success of Smartypants, a quiz game for the Wii. Its broad age appeal and single-purpose concept would pave the way for his iPhone thinking. "The distinctive thing about Smartypants was that it was a very simple idea for a very specific audience—we were trying to build a game to play with our kids, and that didn't exist," he says. His company partnered with Young's Electronic Arts—their first close collaboration after an 18-year friendship. "We built the game in six months for less than a million bucks and it made a lot of money," he says. The game presented players with Trivial Pursuit-style question rounds, with each question tailored to the age of the player. That meant that adult could play with a 16-year-old and an 8-year-old and not be bored. Fast build time was an obvious lesson: after releasing Armed and Dangerous for the Xbox a few years earlier and seeing a tepid consumer response, Stevenson thought, "I'd really like to make faster and cheaper games, so we've got less risk—so we're not spending two years on something that's costing 5 to 10 million dollars, and then finding out in one weekend whether it's going to be successful." But the more significant lesson was in the way that Stevenson thought about his market. Instead of envisioning a target consumer, he and his team had envisioned a playing scenario: parents and kids, together in front of a Wii. The concept of the three-minute "free cycle" that inspired Topple's gameplay harkens back to just that kind of thinking: with iPhone OS gaming, the setting and the players are no longer a foregone conclusion.

Ma, Topple 2's associate and overseer, is perhaps the Topple 2 team's most dedicated gameplayer—though he had never worked on a game before being hired away from a job as a web developer at Yahoo. He says he favors first-person shooters and real-time strategy games, and spends most of his time on Steam.

"These days, I wish I was back in the old days of high school or college, where you had lots of time to play games—you could really get into a deep, immersive experience," he says. "I still feel strongly about the deep experience, but now I'm focused on the immersive experience that comes really quickly, and ends kind of quickly, too. I like that I get that accomplishment of finishing the game without having to take forty to eighty hours on the game." He says that making games relatively easy to beat also encourages players to come back and start all over. "Short games like Call of Duty: Modern Warfare are set up to play out like a movie; it's something like four or five hours long, but it was extremely rewarding, and every level was done really well," he says, citing one example. "And I actually played that game three times through—not in a row, but I've gone back so much because it's such a short experience and it was so enjoyable to do it again, much in the same way you would like pick up a DVD and watch it again."

Bureaucracy and Lightheartedness

While other iPhone developers—in this book and elsewhere—have reported confusing experiences with Apple's app approval process, Stevenson says that dealing with Apple was actually pleasant in comparison with some other console-makers, who primarily cater to large game publishers. "If you're an independent developer like we were, you really have to work hard at your relationships with these [game] companies, because the process can get bureaucratic really easily," says Stevenson. "In particular with Sony. We switched the company over to the PSP, and we were passionate about making something interesting for it. But we found that the help given by Sony at the time was just nonexistent." Compared to Sony, Apple has done "a really great job," says Stevenson. "When we went through the [Sony] approval process, they were so unwelcoming—and I knew some really senior people. I used to have to kind of call in a favor now and then and say 'can you write a message to these [approval] guys and tell them we're not trying to do something bad here?' That we're actually trying to make something good for their platform, and that they should lighten up?" Stevenson recalls. "It was almost like going through customs."

Sony's indifference, Stevenson says, isn't any inherent fault in the company; it's just the laziness that came with the success of the PS2. "Whoever's at number one doesn't usually try hard with the developers," he says. As Apple's dominance of the smartphone app market grows, developers may come to an inflection point at which Android, BlackBerry, or webOS development become more personable and gratifying. That, Stevenson says, was exactly the scenario that he found himself in as an Xbox developer. "Sony existed in contrast with Microsoft, which for a company with their reputation was unbelievably helpful," he says. "They were supportive; they'd send people down to help you with your code, they had an entire team of people that would spend time at the end of a project optimizing your project, so that your game would look better—and they did it for free," Stevenson says. Though Apple has treated Ngmoco well, smaller, less serious shops might find the iPhone to be more hostile terrain. "We were funded quite quickly, so we hired phenomenal staff and engineers, and so we really had a good relationship with Apple because we were treating their device and their market seriously," Stevenson says. "I'd say we've had a slightly different experience than the one or two developers in the bedroom." As of this writing, Ngmoco has no plans to expand to other platforms.

But being bigger than a one-man show takes planning, especially for game publishers, who need to orchestrate art and engineering. "Making sure that you're conveying the technical specifications for the art is really, really helpful to the artist," says Ma. "We had art come in [for Topple 2] and when we put it in the game we needed to stretch it out—it was too small. Unfortunately, the artist was in a time crunch, so he didn't think to start with something bigger and shrink it down," he says. "So then he had to go and start over, and basically recreate it again." Even more crucial to gameplay, Ma says, is music choice. "Working at Ngmoco really made me start appreciating audio, effects and music on levels that I never had in games before," he says. "When you first work on a game there's no music or sound effects yet," he says, "and then suddenly you add them, and it's like a completely different game." For Topple 1, the team added what Ma calls a

"Danny Elfman kind of experience": a kind of grand, orchestral techno type of sound. "But you know, for Topple 2 we ended up on this like Law & Order kind of feel. And, yeah, it totally changed the way you felt about the. The music was huge."

Free vs. Paid

One of the features that sets Topple 2, and other Ngmoco games, apart from their competitors is the way it uses analytics. Those "awesomes" the company monitored in Mazefinger weren't just fanciful indicators of the game's popularity – they were real tools that Stevenson and his team used to make sure the game was at its optimal playability. "From day one we were building a network," Stevenson says. "It was important that we had real-time analytics in all our games, so that we could make them better." In Stevenson's mind, 'real-time' didn't just apply to the downstream data; he wanted real-time game improvement, too. "With Topple and Mazefinger, we could see how far people were getting in the game, and change the skill level on some of the later levels to make sure that people could get through the game."

Though Topple 1 and Mazefinger were treated the same, they were conceived for different purposes. "We released one for free and one paid, because we wanted to understand how the economics worked," says Stevenson. "We thought they were both really good games, and we wanted to see what happens when one goes in free." Both of them shot into the top five games within a day, but because Mazefinger was free, it had ten times as much traffic. "It broke our network," says Stevenson.

It taught Stevenson a valuable lesson. Originally, he had assumed Ngmoco could charge $9.99 for its games, but the success of Mazefinger suggested that the road to profit on the iPhone isn't sales—it's marketshare. "Free games get so much more attention," he says, and in the world of iPhone gaming, attention is the name of the game. Since gaming is the only major genre that Apple itself has stayed out of, no one developer has any technical advantage; it's the freest of the App Store's competitive markets. The result has been explosive growth, fueled in part by Apple's game-centric iPod Touch advertisements. To rise above the rabble, Ngmoco has a plan: "In the future, we are going to be releasing DS-quality games for free," says Stevenson. "This is going to cause a minor freak-out in the industry.

Ngmoco's games will still be sold for money, but they'll also have completely free versions designated "Plus+" that users can download for free. Plus+ (pronounced "plus-plus") is a network that Ngmoco hopes will keep players tied into its games, and more amenable to playing new ones. It requires signing up for a free Plus+ account, which pulls you into a network of other Plus+ gamers that you can compete with. There, you create an avatar, compete on the leaderboards, challenge other players, and broadcast your high scores on Twitter and Facebook. (The Plus+ leaderboard, Figure 3–6.)

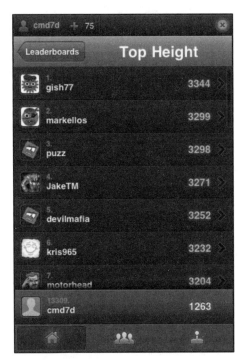

Figure 3–6. *The Plus+ leaderboard tracks a player's progress in all Plus+ games combined.*

The Plus+ network isn't just limited to Ngmoco; the company has also developed an SDK for other game-makers that want to join up. At first, the company will accept Plus+ partners on a case-by-case basis, but later the SDK will become open and available to any game developer that wants to join. Not only will small-time developers get access to Ngmoco's network of points, challenges and playability, they'll also be able to use the company's metrics and promotions engines.

But building the Plus+ network come at a substantial risk. Already, millions of people have paid money for games that have since been made free—a textbook way to make otherwise enthusiastic customers bitter. Asking players to sign up and divulge information is another hurdle. Still, by building a network, Ngmoco will reduce the App Store's already-low friction between downloading, playing, and making in-app purchases—one of the company's planned conduits for revenue. Stevenson says he envisions more future games that are downloadable and playable for free, but that give players the option of buying additional features in-game to change the experience, much like the buying experience inside other social games.

Despite all the potential for market share and upside, the Ngmoco team is still possessed of a humble impulsion. "I feel like from a really young age when I started playing games, I realized I wanted to change the rules," says Ma. "I found a lot of enjoyment not only from playing games but from also creating a different kind of game for other people, and just having other people be happy felt great. That's why I think I always wanted to be a game maker."

Chapter 4

Q&A: Foursquare

Developer Name: Dennis Crowley and Naveen Selvadurai
Development Company: Foursquare
Tags: Visual Design; Connectivity; Client App; Workflow
URL: http://foursquare.com

Foursquare is a location-based social networking game that lets users "check-in" at venues and meet up with friends nearby (Foursquare for iPhone is shown in Figure 4–1). The app handily combines everything from Core Location to push notifications, and its ambitions run deep. It aspires to be a multipurpose tool for socializing, complete with Yelp reviews, maps, nearby tweets, and user profiles. Despite its breadth, Foursquare maintains an economically-designed interface that makes the iPhone's screen feel bigger than it is.

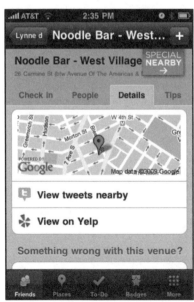

Figure 4–1. *Foursquare's careful tabbed interface packs data into a friendly format.*

Dennis Crowley and Naveen Selvadurai are Foursquare's founders, and built Foursquare for iPhone as a team. Determined to build their app as a standalone tool discrete from Foursquare.com, Crowley and Selvadurai had to navigate not only technical challenges but social consequences, privacy concerns, and new-user foibles. Tempted to explore new UI elements but wary of scaring off new users, the pair has settled on a solid, accessible design after studying some of the iPhone's UI experimenters—two of whom are featured elsewhere in this book.

Crowley is also the founder of a similar service called Dodgeball, which he and a partner sold to Google in 2005. In addition to its iPhone iteration, Foursquare is available as an Android app and on other phones via an SMS interface.

What was your plan for Foursquare for iPhone, and how did you divide the work?

Dennis: We knew we wanted to reproduce some of the features of Dodgeball, like the fun-finder stuff. We knew conceptually that we wanted to make a smarter city guide. I don't think we've fleshed out all the conceptual hurdles yet. But we did a lot of paper mockups, sketching things out on paper. Naveen has a pretty good sense for interaction and design, so we just ran with a lot of that stuff; he was building much of the iPhone stuff, and I was building the backend that would talk to the database. My work figured out how [Foursquare] would spit out a bunch of data and he'd find a way to look it pretty on the iPhone.

Is there a governing aesthetic?

Dennis: We're trying to make it look different than other apps, and trying to find an aesthetic that we like.

Naveen: Having a slightly different look is important to making [Foursquare] a standout among all the other apps in the space. But it's not just to make it look different; the other factor is that we have so much information to cram on the screen. To show a lot of different types of content, we had to introduce some new styles. You don't necessarily want to load all that data onto the same screen—even though we probably could've done that—so we tried to set different priorities, since people place different weight on different types of information.

For instance, for the user profile: you probably take a look at the badges tab maybe a tenth of the time you do one of the other primary tabs. So we realized it has to be cleanly pushed into some sort of side-loader section.

On the home screen, we decided the Check In button and the Shout button have to be central. Not only does that show you information about yourself, and kind of give you a list of all your friends nearby, but we realized that we needed a direct call to action. Front and foremost is the idea of checking in, because without checking in, you're not going to get any of the other candy, you're not going to be able to meet up with your friends, or you're not going to be able to earn badges, and so on.

Do you each have varying ideas about what information the user should be presented with first?

Naveen: We do. One issue is the case of new users vs. experienced users, and that's some of the stuff that we're iterating on right now. We put this [UI] together kind of selfishly—we built it for our friends, and all those use-cases always involve, say, ten or twenty friends. In other words, we built for people who already had Foursquare friends. We realized after we got it out and after we started using it, that most users had only like five friends, maybe ten at most, so we needed to make the experience really good for them at the same time.

Your app relies heavily on tabs to sort information. Is this a good long-term solution?

Dennis: We're going through a UX redesign now. Those tabs are going to look a little bit nicer. We're trying to do a lot in the app. In fact, we might actually be doing too much; we've got tabs in the bottom, tabs in the middle of the screen. All users have been able to understand it, I don't think it's a huge technical challenge, whether it's exactly the right UX for that experience, I'm not sure. Some of the stuff we were just racing to get done as quickly as possible [for South by Southwest] but a good 90% of it is pretty solid and pretty functional.

Naveen: I actually had screenshots of every positive development. The tabbed browsing was there from the beginning—I don't even remember if there was a version before the tab browsing where we tried to cram everything onto a single list. I think the way it worked, we realized, was our menu screen had to have the ability to check in the ability to see all that related stuff. But on the menu page users also want to see details: they wanted to see a map, they wanted to see Yelp information, or which friends are at [a venue].

So what are our options? We can either give them a button or some sort of table show that is basically built into the view, and which basically says "tap here for more details." Or we can adopt some sort of tab approach. We knew we were going to have many styles of data in the future, like a People tab in the menus, so we opted for the latter.

Did any apps serve as inspiration for Foursquare's interaction design?

Dennis: The Facebook app, of course. And the apps that come free on the device, like the ones that most people are used to playing with. Naveen and I have been going through and looking at the latest round of Twitter clients, looking at some what some of the clever UI looks like, and salivating over some of it, and wanting to build it in. Apple's re-standardizing a lot of their UI, because a lot of it has to go. The question is, should we build that new stuff in? Do people understand how to use it?[1]

---

[1] To read more about Facebook for iPhone, turn to Chapter 2.

Naveen: I think Facebook still continues to standout in a good way, cause they have very similar structured data in many different buckets, so to speak. One bucket of data is the user's profile, one bucket of data is the user's News Feed, and so on—we're very similar in that sense.

I would also say that some of the elements in Tweetie are really nice, but what I think what's really confusing about Tweetie [2] is that it breaks the model of the navigation bar at the bottom. One of the best parts about the toolbar is that there's a definite hierarchy, there are definite stacks, as soon as you tap any button in the toolbar, it'll automatically bring you back to the superview of that tab. But what Tweetie has done is take that idea of the toolbar, and break that hierarchy, so the tabs are very much topic-sensitive; you can't really tap to go to the superview. I find it actually to be more difficult to follow than all the other apps, because the hierarchy works when you're drilling into it, but there's no way to come back to the top of the view to see all of my replies, or to see all of my public online views. Maybe it's because I'm a developer and I'm focused on the code [behind] the tab approach.[2]

Dennis: The new Tweetie does have a lot of cool stuff—there's a little widget on the 140-character thing where you flip it and the screen pops up with a bunch of different options; there's the pull down the screen to refresh which we both like. There's another application called StarMap that is really great. It's an astronomy program, it turns the standard five-tab thing at the bottom of the screen so you can rotate it, which is kind of hot. So because you can swivel it to see different views, you basically get 20 buttons instead of 5 buttons.

Naveen: I think Joe [Hewitt] has really solved some navigation problems really well, with the grid [button] at the top, which allows you to get to whatever view you want to. I should add that one of the things I really appreciate about both Tweetie 2.0 and Facebook is that they preserve not only all of your data, but the path you took to get to that data. Your entire path into a view stack is saved. That's part of what makes those apps so fast and so efficient.

You use a lot of Apple's frameworks. Why not source some of the work out to Apple's built-in apps?

Naveen: The more I started using the app, the more I realized there's a lot of value in keeping the user within our app as much as possible. It makes the experience easier. So there's more value in me being able to say, "Oh my friend is hanging out at this bar downtown, Where is it?" And tap into a map in the app.

I can also see Yelp data from within the app, and I can see tweets nearby. I think it's kind of powerful because it keeps me in that mode of, "I'm looking at foursquare data right now," and I am not tempted to jump contexts. If the users really want to jump out of our local native maps into the native Maps app, or if they really wanted to jump out of the built-in tweet view into the native tweet view, they have that option. But I'm trying to avoid that if possible, because I feel once you jump out of the app your train of thought

---

[2] To read more about Tweetie, and Loren Brichter's rebuttal to this critique, turn to Chapter 1.

is broken, and it's harder to jump back in. Figure 4–2 shows Foursquare's in-app tweet stream, based on WebKit.

Now that you've cranked out your initial versions, how do you go about revising the interface?

Dennis: There are certain screens in the app that we want to target first. The screens with a lot of data on them—where we did the bare minimum of design—we need to come back and really revisit. Our strategy is generally to do things piece by piece. A couple of screens will get redesigned and then a couple more in the next revision, and then after two or three more builds the whole thing will look totally different. First and foremost, what we're trying to do is cut down the number of tabs and taps that get you to do whatever you want to do in the app.

Is it better to have more tabs and a cleaner interface, or fewer tabs and a more crowded screen?

Dennis: I think over time different UIs from different apps have helped teach people how to use apps differently. So rather than just having one row or one data element represented by one tab, you can now have multiple tabs in a specific row, with different items you can click on. I know people are doing more complex stuff as people are getting more comfortable with the iPhone UX. I think users are becoming experts at it. I don't know if we're the app to start inventing new UX widgets, but the apps that have a critical mass of users, like the Facebook app and Tweetie and some of these other clients with a large number of users, they can progressively expand. We might inherit ideas from those guys.

Foursquare seems to rely heavily on WebKit. Why?

Dennis: A lot of the stuff we built in to the app was done with WebKit so that we could change it very quickly with HMTL, and not have to create updates for the app. That's how the Leaderboard works. It's also much faster for us to develop that way.

Naveen: The Leaderboard is a great example, because we weren't sure at the time how we were going to reveal stats about a user, but we knew there was going to be this "leader board" concept that compared your points to your friends. We were playing with the idea of using pie charts to display the data. We figured it would be a little more dynamic if we could control it all on the server.

Figure 4–2. *Foursquare's app uses WebKit to allow its builders to iterate without resubmitting their app, and to keep users inside from jumping out to another program.*

Though Foursquare definitely has a unique visual design, Apple inspired some of the smaller details, didn't it?

Dennis: Yeah it did, with their App Store [Buy Now] buttons. We handed those off to our designer, and she came back with little tweaks to it. I think when you look at some of the sizing of those smaller elements, how they are supposed to work, and the minimal font size, I think it's safe to assume that Apple probably nailed it the first time, so we use them as inspiration or guidance on how those things should look or be sized.

Naveen: That was actually one of the points I was debating, like how would I show that button. I definitely did not want to show a native button, and I did not want to make a UI table button. I looked around for a little bit and I realized Apple had come up with this new style approach, this "call to action" button, you could almost call it. In almost every case we only use one of those on any screen, and they almost always use one per item sort of thing.

Certain screens of your app contain "help" text. How do you decide where and when to include those instructions?

Dennis: Some of it comes from user experience and user feedback, where people are like, "I don't know what to do with this page" or, "This didn't act the way I expected it to." And that's just from aggressively testing with our friends and listening to their feedback. I think one of the things we're missing in the app is the welcome screen or the walkthrough process, and that's something you'll see in the next build or the next two builds, where we hold users by the hand and turn them from newbies into users.

Naveen: I think the only two places we really had any help text are the two places that I felt that people would be turned off by a function, either because of privacy issues, or from an annoyance standpoint.

The first place we use [help text] is when you add a friend; we make it known when you add a friend that your phone number and your email are shown to them by default. We wanted to make that clear there because we got a lot of complaints from users who particularly just added anyone and everyone, and complaints from them that, "Hey they can see my phone numbers, what's going on?" And our approach is that it's just easier to have their phone number—they're your friends, so you should be able to call them and you should be able to go out and meet up with them. It's like a Facebook-style approach. On Facebook, if you're friends with someone, of course you should be able to email them. But we realized well we're not like Facebook, we're not that big, so we can't just get away with doing it without letting the user know.

The second instance we [used help text] was right after push notification was launched. We wanted to be one of the first apps to use push, to really use it reliably, because we realized that push is very valuable for an app like ours; it buzzes in your pocket if you have a friend nearby. Of course power users were concerned—the people with 50 or 100 friends in there—that they would get very annoyed very quickly if they got a buzz in their pocket for everyone of their 50 friends. So we made very clear our rules behind pings and how we handle them: we basically said, "Hey, do you want to turn push off for everyone, or do you want to turn it off for an individual user?" Then we told them, "Here's how you do it." We had to be very clear and explicit about that because it's a feature that we launched after the fact. In other words, it's a feature that will sneak onto people's phones through an update, so they may not realize it, and all of a sudden they are going to get these messages.

Not only did we put the help text in the app, but also alongside the update for the app. We sent out an email newsletter with the app that basically said, "By the way, you're going to notice this, but it's going to give you hints on how to get fewer messages, or how to make these messages a little more valuable." Then we actually set up a web page on our site that went into how do you most effectively manage 15 ping requests from your friends—[questions] along those lines.

Do you use any wider system for collecting feedback?

Dennis: No, I haven't looked at the iTunes reviews or anything in a long time. We use a system called GetSatisfaction to collect feedback from users, it's actually really fantastic. We're horribly far behind in the queue, but it's great for aggregating and stuff, we find that a lot of users are helping other users, too.

Did you assume that Foursquare for iPhone users had seen the Web service first?

Naveen: I don't know what to think. I know a lot of people use something like Twitter, and go to the web site for Twitter, and Facebook, too. Based on that, I didn't think the app would be this powerful where people would be experiencing [Foursquare] on the iPhone first. A lot of our close friends hardly ever go to the web site. And we don't really push them to the web site; we want to build as much of the core experience into the app as possible. But I still find it really surprising. I ran some numbers the other day, and I realized that a lot of people that use the app use exclusively the app—it's like they don't even know the web site exists.

Dennis: We kind of had intuited this when we were building things, so we built in a sign up process. So this is totally opposite what Facebook does; Facebook's first "in" is through the web site, and there's nothing else you can do. Sometimes I wish we had that kind of power, because we'd be able to collect data; people are more likely to type in their full names, phone numbers, email addresses, gender, and age on a web site.

Do you take user's real-world behavior into account when you're adding features?

Dennis: We've definitely learned some things since Dodgeball. Initially you'd get check-ins from all of your friends across all cities, and you'd be like, "Why would I care what coffee shop my friend is at in San Francisco?"

We realized that it's not like collecting friends on Facebook—there's some kind of consequence to having too many friends, so we had build in a graceful way to say, "Okay, I want to be friends with you, but I don't want you to see my location." We call those "ex-girlfriend" bugs. There are situations like this that come up all the time; it's really interesting and fascinating stuff to play with.

There are all also all these odd niche behaviors that happen within Foursquare that we're learning from. We'll have people that check in early at a place so they can draw a crowd there, and we'll have people that check in after they leave, because they still want to get the points but they didn't want anyone to show up while they're there. We have people that check in across time, so they can brag about places we know they weren't at. At the same time, there are people checking in at obscure places to throw people off their course. There's all sorts of weird stuff that goes on. On the data side we can tell, but we really don't care what people use this for; if people want to use it to mask their location, that's an important part.

But it's different when you start adding the points, rewards badges, mayors and the other [game] stuff. We're working on is finding a way to say, "You're a little bit too far away from the coffee shop, so we'll tell your friends you're there, but we're not going to give you any points for it." Figure 4–3 shows Foursquare's list of nearby places.

Figure 4–3. *Foursquare shows you what's nearby, and lets notify your friends—or throw them off your trail.*

Do you try to think one step ahead of Apple? Or take their iPhone OS revisions as they come?

Dennis: I think we're pretty reactive. I think both of us are pretty proficient at UX stuff, but we're not visionaries in it, and we'd prefer to leave the experimenting to Apple and a bunch of the other apps that have extremely talented UX people. Through that evolution, we'll pick the UX elements that we decided are the most interesting or the most relevant to our stuff.

Some of the things we've deliberately stayed away from: anything that involves the auto-rotation of the phone, just because we both are not huge fans of it. We also haven't looked at doing [geo-location] maps because we didn't want people to just be dots on a map, initially; we wanted people to see past that. But now it's at the point where I think we should build that stuff in because it really enhances the experience.

What were some of the fights you had over user experience?

Dennis: Naveen and I are always arguing back and forth about what the next version of the product is going to look like and what screens take priority. I think the most recent one was about Apple's pull-down search menus? They're kind of hidden; you have to scroll down until they appear. We were arguing whether that is standard UI, and whether people understand how to use that yet. I'm saying it's not implicit, and Naveen is saying it is. It's one of those things where we'll probably build it in and run it by a bunch of people. A lot of our changes come from very informal user testing.

Naveen: Regarding the search bar being hidden, I want to follow that path because Apple has already done it. They set the precedent, so people are going to be responding to that. I think it works well because it saves those 50 pixels in height, or whatever it is, and it cleans up the interface a little bit. But it is more of a power user thing, and I understand we have to build the app for both newbies and power users.

In fact, you could argue we have to build it more for the newbies than the power users.

Part III

Using Compression to Cram More Data into a Local App–Large Images, Geo Data, and Lots of It

Who says that a small computer has to run small apps?

Certainly no one at Intermap, makers of AccuTerra. This GPS-mapping app offers thousands of square miles of hyper-detailed maps for iPhone users to examine, breadcrumb, mark, and explore. Luckily for AccuTerra's developers, Intermap already had all that map data ready--but it was no small challenge to slice it all into palatable, usable parcels and then find a way to monetize the various parts.

Jonathan and Ashley Wegener, who built Exit Strategy NYC, faced the opposite situation: a dead-simple idea for a useful app that required three months of subway-riding just to collect the data that would be their core asset.

While both apps make good case studies in image compression, data handling, memory management, and pricing, what makes them most interesting from a developer point of view is the ambition behind their designs. Exit Strategy NYC went from being a nifty but nichey subway app to a full-blown transit-map compendium that appeals to even the most seasoned Gotham resident. AccuTerra improves the original conceit behind GPS apps--"you are here"--by adding additional layers of information: hydrological information, route maps, elevation, weather and a planned implementation of augmented reality on top of it all.

What keeps these apps happily earthbound and ultimately so useable, is both developers' keen adherence to carefully-planned release strategies. They've started with the bare minimum, and tolerated the customer complaints and one-star reviews, all in the name of iterative design. It's not just design but patience, their stories suggest, that is crucial to making a data-heavy app possible and profitable.

Chapter 5

AccuTerra

Developer Name: Dave Witonsky and Randall Barnhart
Development Company: Intermap
Tags: Compression; Efficient Code; Release Strategy
URL: http://accuterra.com/

"We have roughly 170 products on the shelf today," says Dave Witonsky, head of smartphone development for Intermap. He's not talking about apps. He's talking about in-app purchase items: hyperdetailed maps that users can buy and download as they travel. Welcome to the dizzying world of AccuTerra: the iPhone's titanic terabyte app (see Figure 5–1).

Figure 5–1. *"I want this app to help people plan their trips, view their trips, and share them. I want it to enhance that experience of being in the outdoors," says Witonsky.*

Unlike the rest of the apps profiled in this book, AccuTerra, which won the ADA for beta use of iPhone OS 3.0, was awarded an Apple Design Award not for what it did, but for what it has the potential to do. And although Intermap's app is now in the App Store, it's still AccuTerra's incredibly ambitious roadmap that sets it apart from the crowd. And although not every developer has access to the mapping data from a multimillion-dollar navigation company, AccuTerra shows how developers of all stripes can build massive data-intensive apps—and do it profitably.

Building a Framework

Intermap is not just an iPhone development shop; it's a map-data provider. "We have flown all over the U.S. and western Europe to collect highly detailed mapping and elevation information," Witonsky explains, "and we have very accurate models of the earth that contract out to governments, flight insurance companies, and OEM personal navigation companies." Intermap, in other words, is not your average Mac shop that has decided to tool around with a new platform. In building a deeply complex app, they have a lot at stake.

NEXTNat, the company's name for its map data, gets around because of its level of detail: automotive, trucking, and flight companies use Intermap's data because it includes elevation, hydrological data, and other matrices of info. Witonsky says that Intermap saw that personal navigation devices were giving way to smartphones, and they figured they could ditch the middlemen—companies that make personal navigation devices—and bring their data straight to consumers. "So we built early prototypes for the iPhone, and of course, this tsunami of popularity came," Witonsky says.

As the iPhone proliferated, the scope of Intermap's app expanded. "We focused first on national park trails and research, and then pulled these trails and description and attributes from guidebooks and other public sources," Witonsky says. Then his team consolidated and verified their data, and started working on making the rest of the nation's detailed maps available, too. Witonsky wants AccuTerra to someday be a one-stop outdoor guide for the entire contiguous Untied States. "Eventually I'll be able use the app to put in, say, Mars, Colorado, and choose [trails of] moderate difficulty," he says. "Then let's say I'd rather not see what's called tight-usage, or trails with horses and mountain bikers on it; I'd rather just hikers-only. The way we're building this thing, we can provide them two or three choices based on our algorithm. The next thing the person will want to know is the 3D profile, which will leverage our NEXTNat high-resolution elevation model. They can see how steep a trail is." Figure 5–2 shows AccuTerra's information dashboard.

Figure 5–2. *AccuTerra pays attention to all the available data about your trip recording.*

As opposed to some of the other navigation apps that leverage Google Maps or Open Street maps, AccuTerra uses all of Intermap's own map data. "Other apps could integrate to the MapKit framework and get things out faster," Witonsky says. "Our value-add, a big one, is that we're onboard. We used our own mapping framework; we built it from scratch."

"We did take a lot of cues from MapKit," says Randall Barnhart, the lead developer of Intermap's five-man team. "And we do also use MapKit to interface with Google, so that we can provide people who are doing recordings in an urban area with the option of using Google maps instead [of Intermap's] if they want." But building their custom map-kit was the brunt of the work behind the app. "It was an absolutely massive undertaking," Witonsky says.

Intermap's other killer feature is detail. But being able to fetch a detailed map of every square mile of the U.S. requires a lot of images—far too many for a single app, or even for a dozen apps. The team decided to build an in-app map store so that users could buy detailed maps as they needed them over their 3G connection, delete old ones if they needed space, and re-download the ones they've already bought. Along the way, they had to figure out how to mate their purchasing back-end with Apple's, and how to deliver gigabytes of map data over the air.

Divide and Conquer

Apple's terms and conditions require that all in-app purchases go through the App Store. There are ways around that—several e-book apps have eschewed the rule—but Witonsky thought it better to stay on Apple's good side if his company was going to pour so much money and effort into their app. But following the rules meant that map downloads and payments would have to take a convoluted route.

"We made the decision that we were going to rasterize all of these trails and all the different levels of detail—hydrology layers and so on—all in the raster image," Witonsky says. "When these maps raster, when you start talking about an entire state, the country, earth, this stuff is heavy. Even if you're using PVRTC, if you're at high-resolution these things are 512kb per tile. It adds up real quickly."

Had they packaged the entire app with every available U.S. map, Witonsky says, it would have been well over a terabyte. "We considered going out the door with different states bundled with our application," he says. "Each bundle, of course, would be one app on the App Store that we could charge someone $10.00 for. By the time we split up all the states, and the larger states into sections, lo and behold, we were up to 70 bundles. It was just too confusing." IPhone OS 3.0 brought in-app purchasing, saving Intermap from having to inundate the App Store. Instead, it built a map store inside AccuTerra. "We figured we could release this one app, and sell the other maps piecemeal—though the basic app is a bit heavy at 110MB because it contains continental data. But on top of that, we figured we could side load these other contents: your wide-area maps, big states, national parks and recreational areas." (Figure 5–3, AccuTerra's pre-installed "continental" view of New York.)

Figure 5–3. *AccuTerra provides users with an overall view, but for more detail, additional maps must be purchased.*

AccuTerra's map store is entirely separate from the App Store, but it must communicate with Apple's servers to coordinate purchases. To make the hand-off fluid, Intermap's engineers designed their in-app catalog to be consonant with the Apple experience. "The map store is highly modeled on the actual App Store itself," says Barnhart, who began his career at defense contractor Raytheon doing Java work application development. "How we categorize products, how we have these table views; how you tap a row, get more information about it, or go down a level; we're using a lot of the built in UI-kit user interface to do a lot of the same things that you'd see in Apple native apps," he says.

In-app purchases in AccuTerra deliver tiles of a region in various resolutions: the medium-quality Continental maps are what Intermap calls 32-degree/8-degree/2-degree-quality images, and the higher definition maps, used in parks and recreational areas, are designated 30-minute/7.5 minute/2.5 minute images. "That is a full stack stored locally, so when you pinch and zoom, you're not connected over 3G or WiFi," says Witonsky. "This is a huge thing for us, because our maps are resident on the device, unlike Google Maps which come in over the network."

The levels of detail depend on the area a user buys. If you in-app purchase a state, and you get the 30 minute and 7.5 minute-level of detail; when they get the national parks and other high-use recreational areas, you get 2.5 minute-level maps, which are higher resolution. Future versions of AccuTerra will go even more in-depth. "We're creating version 2.0 of AccuTerra, which will have more trails, better roads, everything—and for that we're creating all new 30s, all new 7.5s, and 2.5s for the whole U.S.," Witonsky says. Translation: the app's enormous 400-600MB maps are getting even heavier.

Witonsky says he'll solve the problem by making the app-buying location-aware: drive to a trail-head and the app gives you the option of downloading a map of the five square miles around you. "This is where on-demand buying becomes appealing," Witonsky says. "If we split the maps into five-square-mile tiles, each one ends up less than 10MB and I can download it via 3G or EDGE." Figure 5–4 shows a list of maps available for sale.

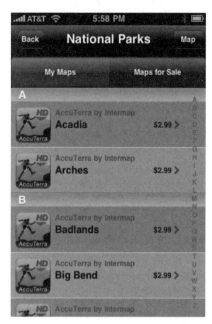

Figure 5–4. *A list of maps for sale inside AccuTerra.*

Building an In-App Store

Apple's restrictions made AccuTerra's massive in-app catalog a peculiar task. Because the maps are what Apple deems a "non-consumable" product, Intermap has to register each purchase on its server, so that the system knows which maps a user has bought, and won't make him pay if he wants to download that same map again. But because Intermap can't access a user's iTunes account name for privacy reasons, they have to ask each customer to sign up with new credentials on a separate Intermap system. "There's a real twist when it comes to managing your content, because as the developer I have to give you the ability to uninstall a given state map to free up space," Witonsky says. "But I have to list that map in my store as 'uninstalled' status so that you can get that map again. But because StoreKit doesn't track your purchases, at first the App Store doesn't know you already purchased this state. So we have to pop up a little alert, and say, 'Hey, if you bought this under the same iTunes account, you're not actually going to be charged, even though the in-app store says 'buy,'" he explains. "Once you hit 'buy' again, we get that transaction, we know you already bought it, and our server sends it back to your phone for free. That's how you have to manage selling a large set of data." Figure 5–5 shows a catalog listing for the New York State map; Figure 5–6 shows a map's coverage area.

Figure 5–5. *State and regional maps vary in price and size.*

Barnhart says the trickiest part was keeping the sets of information straight. "Developing the in-app store capability raised a lot of issues, since we have our own server that keeps track of users and what map they've downloaded," he says. "But at the same time, there's Apple's framework StoreKit, which also enabled the e-commerce transaction to take place using the person's iTunes account. So we have a bit of duplicate information there, as far as the names of things purchased. So an interesting thing from our side is that our server has to go out and we look for our list of products, then have to come back and make a request out to Apple to say, 'Okay, which of these products on your side are also signed with the same information and are ready for sale?' Then we use that list to display to the user what is ready for purchase," he says. He contrasts the experience to selling apps for Google's Android platform. "We didn't go out and do our own e-commerce thing, because we were bound by Apple's terms and conditions. But if you go to a different platform like Android, all the people that are doing e-commerce through their app are just essentially connected to their own server."

The in-app purchase system also creates confusion when it comes to documenting purchases—something that is crucial when a user can spend upwards of $200 inside a single app. "There are issues with keeping track of receipts and transactions that Apple has on their side, versus transactions and receipts that we're tracking," Barnhart says. "For example, what happens if someone interrupts the download halfway through? What's the best way for us to resume? Is it to go through Apple and see if they have that same transaction, or should we go through our server side? Or do we go through both?" Eventually, Intermaps' engineers figured out that the best way to handle this scenario was to have the app check for outstanding transactions with Apple. "If it's something that the user pauses or cancels themselves, our app considers [itself] done with the transaction," Barnhart explains. "That said, the user can come back anytime and query our servers and see that, yes, they have this product installed, and they can go ahead and download it for free again without having to go through any kind of iTunes transaction."

Of course, it's not always that easy, says Witonsky. "There's a stumbling block with the way they've set up their [StoreKit] framework that can create problems for users who are resetting their phones, or are trying to transfer data over to new phones," he explains. "It's not a big scenario, but it's a complication. When purchase information is stored in two places, it's harder to make it clear to the user what's happening, and how they can get their data back."

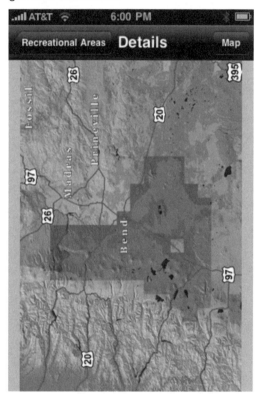

Figure 5–6. *Each map in AccuTerra's store shows you the area of coverage you're buying. This one is of Deschutes River State Recreation Area in Oregon.*

PVRTC or Broke

In Chapter 3, we discussed using PVRTC to compress images economically. For AccuTerra, PVRTC was not only a nice way to cut down on memory-hogging—it was the difference between a usable app and an unusable one. "Because we use PVRTC, we can fit a number of tiles in memory, and therefore the user experience of panning and zooming is much better, because the app doesn't have to go outside the data structure and bring back more tiles," Witonsky explains. But there are always limitations; because the app can't possibly load all the tiles from a given stack, it has to decide which ones take priority. "We developed sophisticated algorithms to manage that which tiles get loaded," he says.

Barnhart says the algorithm essentially tries to predict what area of the map the user will want to see next, and load it in memory. "The algorithm does a lookup based on the screen location reference and finds the appropriate map tile to display at the appropriate scale," he says. Behind the scenes, the app is being judicious about what it loads. "We had to become very knowledgeable about the frameworks, and know how to receive memory warnings from the OS. [The OS] will tell you, 'Hey, you better free up resources you aren't using,' or 'Hey, you better release this.' Handling those warnings challenged us greatly."

The situation became complex when it came time to add ancillary features to the app. "Everyone wants to use the camera inside the app, but through the [camera] framework, Apple takes over memory, then hands you memory back," Witonsky says. "We found that when they handed everything back, we ended up pushing the envelope with memory and we'd have to release view-controllers and everything. We had to go back and work very hard to optimize everything so that other frameworks or background processes wouldn't cause the app to get killed."

Other Apple apps exacerbated the problem. "We kept running into a problem where if someone had loaded up Safari with four or five different web pages, it was caching that information in memory and making our application's available memory space a lot smaller," Barnhart says. "We were running into this issue that when you were recording a trek and you took a picture, like maybe on the fourth or fifth time, our stream would freeze." The engineers realized that their app was being issued memory alerts by the OS when they came close to hitting the limit, but that the app wasn't doing anything with those alerts; it was just logging them and continuing business as usual. "After a lot of debugging, we realized that Apple's framework gives you levels of warning, and if you cross the threshold where there's maybe only 5% available memory for your application, it starts yanking things," Barnhart says. Having camera view on top of map view, a bunch of tiles loaded up, and trip breadcrumbs was too much for the OS to handle. "We came to realize that the view pointer for that view controller was getting yanked out from underneath us from the system, and when it came back from taking the picture, lo and behold, if we were trying to reference a button that was connected to that view, the app would crash."

Lazy Loading

After asking around at WWDC and scouring Apple message boards, Intermap's coders eventually figured out how to handle the low memory conditions the OS was warning them about. The solution: lazy loading.

In the app's initial design, for example, it created its map buttons upon launch, and only did it once. But once memory became low, the OS would pull the root view out from underneath the app in order to prevent a crash. "We came to realize we have to create these buttons as late as possible," Barnhart says, "because there are these other delegate methods that appear that could get called from Apple's API when these events happen in the UI. We realized that you have to initialize these things and wire them up in those instances, so that in the event the root view gets pulled, you can rewire things." Once they began to delay loading, they could load on as many Safari pages or photos as they wanted without a crash.

The trick, Barnhart says, was knowing what to release from memory when resources were low. "We got some advice from Apple engineers to release IB buttons, these special UI objects. At a certain point, Apple will call this message and tell us, 'Okay, we've pulled the root view, you need to try to release as much memory as you can.' Then they essentially call these delegate methods, saying, 'Okay, I'm initializing it; I'll initialize that once.' But every time I show the root view, I'm going to call this other method. That's where we have to wire things up correctly. It was definitely an interesting lesson learned for us."

The other lesson, says Barnhart, was to get to know the IDE tools before mucking through a problem. "Using Instruments to profile memory is absolutely crucial, he says. "I'd say definitely learn that stuff—it's very valuable in tracking down problems, and just to see how your code is performing in general. I would say that's the one skill that will differentiate people who build better apps from the people who don't."

Memory Diagnostics: Sample Project

To easily determine and query current memory within the running app, AccuTerra defines the following functions in our main app delegate class:

```
(declarations)
// system memory query methods
+ (vm_statistics_data_t) retrieveSystemMemoryStats;
+ (int) calcSystemPageSize;
+ (int) calcSystemAvailableMemoryInMB;
+ (int) calcSystemRemainingMemoryInMB;
+ (int) calcSystemPercentFreeMemory;
+ (BOOL) doWeHaveEnoughFreeMemory:(int)numOfBytesRequested;

(implementations)
+ (vm_statistics_data_t) retrieveSystemMemoryStats
{
    mach_msg_type_number_t count = HOST_VM_INFO_COUNT;

    vm_statistics_data_t vmstat;
host_statistics(mach_host_self(), HOST_VM_INFO, (host_info_t)&vmstat, &count);

        return vmstat;
}

+ (int) calcSystemPageSize
```

```
{
        size_t length;
    int mib[6];

    int pagesize;
    mib[0] = CTL_HW;
    mib[1] = HW_PAGESIZE;
    length = sizeof(pagesize);
    sysctl(mib, 2, &pagesize, &length, NULL, 0);

        return pagesize;
}

+ (int) calcSystemAvailableMemoryInMB
{
        int pagesize = [Trek_AppDelegate calcSystemPageSize];
        vm_statistics_data_t vmstat = [Trek_AppDelegate retrieveSystemMemoryStats];

        return ((vmstat.wire_count + vmstat.active_count + vmstat.inactive_count +
vmstat.free_count) * pagesize) / 0x100000;
}

+ (int) calcSystemRemainingMemoryInMB;
{
        int pagesize = [Trek_AppDelegate calcSystemPageSize];
        vm_statistics_data_t vmstat = [Trek_AppDelegate retrieveSystemMemoryStats];

        return ((vmstat.free_count * pagesize) / 0x100000);
}

+ (int) calcSystemPercentFreeMemory
{
        vm_statistics_data_t vmstat = [Trek_AppDelegate retrieveSystemMemoryStats];
        double total = vmstat.wire_count + vmstat.active_count + vmstat.inactive_count +
vmstat.free_count;
    double free = vmstat.free_count / total;

    return (int)(free * 100.0);
}

+ (BOOL) doWeHaveEnoughFreeMemory:(int)numOfBytesRequested
{
        int pagesize = [Trek_AppDelegate calcSystemPageSize];
        vm_statistics_data_t vmstat = [Trek_AppDelegate retrieveSystemMemoryStats];

        if((vmstat.free_count * pagesize) > numOfBytesRequested)
        {
                return YES;
        }
        else
        {
                return NO;
        }
}
```

It then uses these to display in log messages or alerts as follows:

```
/**
```

```
 *       This method handles Check Memory view
 */
- (void) handleCheckMem_View
{
        Log( @"handleCheckMem_View" );
        int availMem = [Trek_AppDelegate calcSystemAvailableMemoryInMB];
        int remainMem = [Trek_AppDelegate calcSystemRemainingMemoryInMB];
        int percentFreeMem = [Trek_AppDelegate calcSystemPercentFreeMemory];
        NSString* memStr = [[NSString alloc] initWithFormat:@"Total Available:
%iMB\nAmount Remaining: %iMB\nPercent Free of Total: %i%%", availMem, remainMem,
percentFreeMem];
        NSString* msg;
        if(remainMem < 5)
                msg = [[NSString alloc] initWithFormat:@"Low memory!\n%@", memStr];
        else if(remainMem < 15)
                msg = [[NSString alloc] initWithFormat:@"Average memory.\n%@", memStr];
        else
                msg = [[NSString alloc] initWithFormat:@"High memory.\n%@", memStr];
        Log(msg);
        // Debug development team detailed low memory message.
        UIAlertView *memalert = [[UIAlertView alloc] initWithTitle:@"Current Memory"
message:msg delegate:self cancelButtonTitle:nil otherButtonTitles:@"OK", nil];
        [memalert show];
        [memalert release];
        [memStr release];
        [msg release];
}
```

Dealing with Low Memory Warnings

The amount of memory available to your application depends upon the device's available runtime memory. The iPhone 3G has 128 MB and the 3GS has 256MG. But because the OS and services like Mail, iPod, and Safari may be running in the background, the amount of memory available to your application on the iPhone 3G usually starts out at between 20 and 60 MB. The OS keeps track of how much memory your app is currently consuming and will try to free memory if it detects your app crossing certain thresholds of memory consumption.[1]

As Apple's documentation says:

At 80% consumption, the OS will issue a memory warning, which your app can respond to by implementing the didReceiveMemoryWarning function in your view controller classes. This gives you an opportunity to try and release any memory that you don't currently need (like things you may be caching).

---

[1] "This document was helpful to us while we were solving memory issues," says Barnhart: http://developer.apple.com/iphone/library/featuredarticles/ViewControllerPGfori PhoneOS/BasicViewControllers/BasicViewControllers.html#//apple_ref/doc/uid/TP40 007457-CH101-SW4

At 90% consumption, the OS will begin to remove memory underneath you. Specifically, if you have views in a stack, any views not visible will have their view pointers reset. Because of this possibility, developers need to handle this situation in two ways.

- Implement viewDidUnload and release any IBOutlets.

- Make sure the creation of your view (any buttons or drawing) occurs as late as possible in the order view creation call hierarchy (awakeFromNib, viewDidLoad, viewWillAppear, viewDidAppear).

Here is how the Intermap developers handled their low memory bug, which was causing the screen to freeze after the user took a photo with the camera while inside AccuTerra. "The view pointer was getting reset causing references to buttons within that view to be bad," explains Barnhart.

In their RootViewController.m class, the root view used for lifetime of app running, the code goes like this:

```
- (void)didReceiveMemoryWarning {

        Log(@"RootviewController::didReceiveMemoryWarning
*********************************");
        if (!didReceiveMemoryWarning)
        {
                if (curlingUp || photoTaken)
                {
                        // Remove all subviews
                }
        }
}

/**
 * Overridden from UIViewController:
 * Called when the controller's view is released from memory
 */
-(void) viewDidUnload
{
        // Release all of our IBOutlets
 }



//called after taking photo as the modal picker is dismissed
-(void) viewDidLoad
{
        [self restoreViewsForLowMemoryWarning];

        [super viewDidLoad];

        // ... more initialization code here ...
}

//may be called many times
- (void)viewDidAppear:(BOOL)animated
{
        Log(@"RootViewController::viewDidAppear");
```

```
        [self restoreViewsForLowMemoryWarning];
        [self.navigationController setNavigationBarHidden:YES animated:NO];

        // ... more initialization code here ...
}

- (void)viewWillAppear:(BOOL)animated
{
        Log(@"RootViewController::viewWillAppear");
        [self restoreViewsForLowMemoryWarning];
        [super viewWillAppear:animated];

        // ... more initialization code here ...
}
```

"This function is important because it is what allows us to reconnect the view pointer that is removed from underneath us with all the elements that critical to showing our main map view," says Barnhart:

```
-(void) restoreViewsForLowMemoryWarning
{
        if (didReceiveMemoryWarning)
        {
                // Create and add subviews
                didReceiveMemoryWarning = NO;
        }
}
```

Building Forward

The Intermap team's accomplishments with AccuTerra pale in comparison to their aspirations. Witonsky says that in subsequent iterations of the app, map graphics will switch to vector drawing, so that users can turn on and off layers of detail and like camp grounds, trailheads, and weather. Users will also be able to toggle between Google Maps and AccuTerra maps, or Google's other views, Satellite and Hybrid.

The goal, Witonsky says, is to be able to start recording a hike in AccuTerra, take pictures, check out a Google map, and continue to keep your breadcrumb trail the whole time. But that's only the beginning. "Version 3.2 is going to allow our users to import and export into all these UGC sites like trails.com, or any site that exposes their API," he says. "Let's say you put in a search for Westchester [New York]; you'll see a list of perhaps 10 trails that users uploaded, and you can download them onto our maps as a layer," he says. "We are also putting a search interface on our maps and a resident database, so when you put in a campground or another POI, it'll find that thing, geocode it to a lat-long location, and easily move you to that location on our map or Google's maps." That, Witonsky says, will allow the map to jump to the location of the thing the user searched for, without the need for scrolling and panning. "That then sets me up for the on-demand purchase interface, for buying that 5 square mile map area of the place you searched for," Witonsky explains. "That's the killer feature."

All that means writing adaptable code. "We've kind of gone over high-level features that are coming down the road, and I tell [my team] to keep in mind: any kind of content could be coming down through the library through an import, whether it be geotagged photo or a geotagged website," Witonsky says. "We've got to keep in mind that when we're designing this next UI, that we have to be able to make it extensible and chock it full of placeholders for all these things that are coming down the road."

What's down the road? Augmented reality. "After version 3.2, 3D will be next, Witonsky says, "and it'll all be tied into this trip planner." The app will contain an algorithm that will take all the parameters of an outdoor trip you want to do—location, length, difficulty, and trail-use type—and show you a list of potential routes. "Once you get the results, you'll be able to do a 3D flyover of the area [on the phone]," Witonsky says. "If you like the area, you can purchase the map bundle, and away you go."

Intermap believes their audience will grow as AccuTerra grows, from outdoors-lovers to history buffs and eventually into the education market. "In my opinion, multimedia is what's really going to win this [augmented reality] fight," Witonsky says. "So not only will you be able to buy a map of a Civil War battlefield, but you'll get audio clips, pictures, text, video and descriptions of trail hikes," he explains. "You could be hiking and there'd be icons that pop up in your view representing a relevant audio or video clip for that spot," he says. "That's the true vision of this product."

Much of that vision will depend on Intermap finding partnerships with content providers, but Witonsky says he's confident the app will progress as planned—and at breakneck speed. "I have a roadmap that in six to nine months that I'm going to have a lot of it done," he says. "This thing is moving so fast that it feels like a tsunami."

Chapter 6

Q&A: Exit Strategy NYC

by Jonathan and Ashley Wegener

Q&A: Exit Strategy NYC
Developer Name: Jonathan and Ashley Wegener
Development Company: JWeg Ventures LLC
Tags: Release Strategy; Outdoing Copycats
URL: http://exitstrategynyc.com/

Exit Strategy NYC (Figure 6–1) is an app built on a big gamble: months of work went into it before any coding began. For developers considering ideas with a lot of sweat equity or real-world overhead—licensing others' content, spending hours on graphic design—the story behind Exit Strategy NYC speaks to one crucial question: is building this app worth it? And if so, how do you scale it into a fully-featured piece of software?

Figure 6–1. *Once you've chosen a line, you can see the most efficient transfer strategy.*

ESNYC began as a simple series of maps that tell New York City subway riders which cars to ride in to make their line-transfers most efficient. (Want to take the L train to the 6 train? Get on the fourth car, and when the doors open, you'll be right in front of the correct set of stairs.) Useful, sure, but also a niche app with limited sales appeal. To gain a following, the brother-sister team Jonathan and Ashley Wegener kept careful focus on their target users, and crafted a careful a press strategy to reach them.

For version 2.0, the pair licensed official New York City subway, bus, and neighborhood maps and turned their app into a comprehensive transit guide for veteran New Yorkers and newbies alike. With a core group of dedicated users ready to sing its praises, ESNYC 2.0 took off to brisk sales and five-star reviews.[1]

You had an app idea that demanded a big time investment, even before programming began. How did you know it'd be worth it?

It took about two and a half months. We mapped pretty much every day, like a nine to five job. We tried to catch at least one of the rush hours—some days we'd start really early and get the morning rush, and other days we'd catch the evening rush hour. We got more done when the trains ran quicker.

We decided it would be worth it, even if it was just for ourselves and nobody in the world bought our app and it made no money. We sort of made up our minds that this was something that we as New Yorkers wanted.

We also knew we'd get a lot of attention from the media, partially because someone had already done this—not in app form, but in book form in Toronto about five or six years ago—and he got a ton of press for it. We were relatively confident that it was a great idea. I remember the moment I first decided to go forward with it: I was spitting out business ideas that I could make [to a friend], and when I mentioned this one he basically told me, "Dude this is an awesome idea, you have to do it!"

New York is a big city, but how did you know there'd be a market to sell to?

I spent a lot of time doing market research, because that's my background. And I basically ran through a whole bunch of market-sizing questions; the [demographic] numbers, how many we expected to sell. By my estimations, the app should have sold about 30,000 copies if everything went perfectly, and it wasn't too far off from that.

Why is this idea best suited for the iPhone?

We realized early on that this information is really most useful in your pocket, rather than a web site or some kind of physical book or something. And the project itself, the idea kind of originated when I started recording this information in the notepad feature of the iPhone. I just kept a notepad where the doors were for my own purposes, because I was

---

[1] To read how Jonathan, Ashley and their developer strategized for version 2.0, check out Chapter 12.

having trouble figuring it out. So one day I just counted, and I was like, okay, fourth car, third door. So I wrote it down. And I just kept adding stations as I went around the city.

The next logical step to keeping track of something in your phone's notebook is: why isn't this an app? This is the type of thing that hopefully you can turn around and sell for 99 cents to a million people and make a million dollars.

How do you handle the database of stops and cars?

In terms of what Exit Strategy actually is, it's really a very low-tech app; it doesn't use any of the features of the phone, it doesn't use audio, video, visual stuff, it doesn't use accelerometer, it doesn't use the GPS, it doesn't use the Internet, it's entirely offline. Really it's a collection of images, it's just … the app is nothing more than a delivery vehicle of data and information, and that information is those little pictures of each little spacing diagram. (See Figure 6–2. In version 1.0, not all subway stops were covered. Wegener completed his database for version 2.0.)

Figure 6–2. *Choose your line...*

When we originally set out to make the app, the original concept was to dynamically draw these cars of the train, and we knew that the number of the cars on the train differed, so you'd either draw eight, nine, ten or eleven, and then dynamically you'd draw the exit to the left of it. The idea was to have a database where we could track for every stop, and have a row in the database for every exit. So like the row would be 42nd street, and then the next column would be the door number, and the car number— something like that.

What we realized when we started sort of making this database was, one, it was going to be incredibly error-prone, trying to enter this information into a database; and two, that we should just use images. Images would be less error-prone, and easier in some ways across platforms. Databases transfer nicely, but images also transfer nicely. (Figure 6–1 shows one such subway image.)

How did you ensure that all these images would load quickly?

Loading the data as an image makes the app faster and more importantly from our aspect is it lowers the development time and cost. If we're shouldering the work of actually of making the little station images, rather than having to paste the info onto some kind of dynamic drawing algorithm, it makes it a very, very simple app. The interface is sort of just a way to give it a hierarchy and a way to access those pictures. We ended up making that change and hiring a graphic designer to come up with the basic train diagram in Illustrator, and then making hundreds of little images. There are 500 hand-drawn station diagrams in the [1.0 version]. That itself took, well, not as long as riding the subway, but at least a week.

How, if at all, can you make this a sustainable business?

That's a really interesting question because I had that exact realization: this could be a real business. When we started this project the aim was really to do a one-shot deal, and make a million dollars, and then retire, or just move on with our lives. The reality of what the sales looked like was at the hump at the beginning, like, we had this major press launch, when we got coverage in every newspaper and magazine in NY basically, and TV stations. The hump, the height of the hump, was less than I expected. It did in the first few days kind of depressingly less than I expected, but the plateau was more than I expected; the plateau sort of meaning the continuous two or three weeks after launch when all the press was dead. That was higher than I expected.

That business is about serving the continuously growing market of new iPhone buyers, and new people discovering our app. And so we're making some changes to make it more of a mass appeal app, and less of a niche New Yorker app. The next version is going to be five dollars.

How do you make your app useful to more people?

First thing we do is add a NYC subway map; we've licensed from the MTA the right to use their maps, their schedules, basically everything from the MTA. We're going to try to make it a premium map that has a ton of great information for New Yorkers about the subway system and the bus system. (Figure 6–3 shows part of the Queens bus map.)

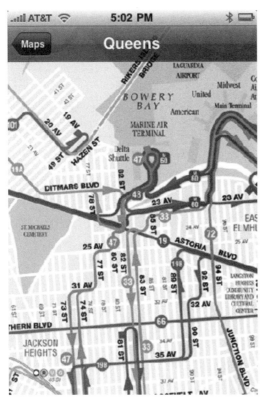

Figure 6–3. *Bus riders are currently underserved by most NYC transit apps, so Wegener hopes including line maps will help set Exit Strategy apart as the most comprehensive of its competitors.*

The maps seem really easy to do—like, "Oh, you just stick in the map," but that takes hours of the programmer's time. It's actually a big technical challenge, because you have a very large image, and you need to tile, you need to cut it into a thousand different pieces and assemble them quickly and easily. So if you see the way iTransit works, it reloads a section the screen very quickly. It took me and the developer I'm working with about a week to get that right, just having a map alone, a beautiful high-res, zoomable, scrollable map.

The MTA has given us a bunch of really cool data, and they've even kind of gone out of their way to grab some extra data. We'll have the subway map, we'll have all five borough bus maps, we will have possibly the Metro North maps, but the coolest thing that we're going to have is the other half of the piece of the puzzle. Right now we have exit data; we tell you how to get off the train, out the station. But what we'll be adding is enter strategy.

Here's what I mean: when you come through the [subway] turnstiles you see a local neighborhood map. We basically have all of those from the MTA, and are going to be integrating those into the map, so at the bottom of the station screen. So if you're going to Bedford on the L, and you're looking at the exit data, there will be a button at the bottom that says, "flip to neighborhood map," and you can press that, it will take you to an above, to a street map image of the neighborhood, as well as MTA's diagram of the station, which shows exactly where the staircases come above ground. Figure 6–4 shows on of MTA's neighborhood maps.

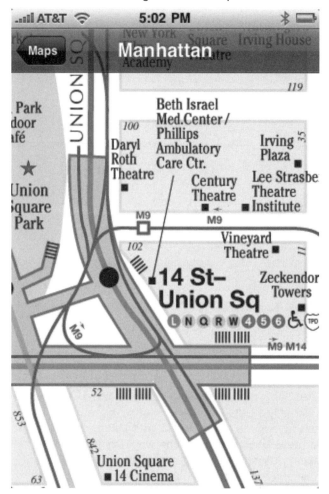

Figure 6–4. *One of the MTA's neighborhood maps, showing entries and local landmarks.*

So the app will become something else entirely—a hyperlocal neighborhood transit map.

It'll all be integrated—you'll basically be able to scroll around the neighborhood and use the MTA's neighborhood map, from your phone. It'll show you what's around that stop. For example, in the case of Manhattan, we had about 20 Manhattan maps, and I basically wove them together into this giant quilt, so now we have coverage of a super giant single map that covers all of Manhattan that has every single subway station, where the exits come above ground, and the bus lines drawn on top of it. It has where the staircases are and where the elevators are for every subway station. Originally they were giant Illustrator files of the maps: 30MB files with 600 layers, with every street name, every letter in the word you can change.

We had to pay the MTA $5,000 to use them; that's 10% of our [projected] profits. (Figure 6-5 shows the official NYC Subway map.)

What about the 10MB download limit over 3G?

That's something I've been thinking a lot about. When we launched the app, we were really concerned about this 10MB threshold. Our app right [in version 1.0] is 6MB with 500 station images; people can impulsively buy it if somebody tells them about it at a party, which is cool. And the other two competitors in the subway map market are both are under 7MB. But there's no way realistically we're going to be under 10MB with the amount of information we want to add [to the next version]. So once you pass that restriction, and that constraint is lifted, we decided you can really go crazy. Once we add all these neighborhood maps, the app will probably be between 50 and 100MB.

Version 1.0 didn't cover every subway station in New York. Is it worth pursuing the "long-tail" customer who wants every corner of a map documented?

We decided we'd rather launch early with less data. The app right now has about maybe 60 or 70% of New York covered; it doesn't do the very end of all the lines in the outer-boroughs. If we had gotten fed up and given up earlier, we would've just launched with less data.

How deep should you drill into the NYC market before moving on to other cities or projects?

By far the biggest market is NYC for anything cool and local. We've had people from Chicago, and Boston, and Washington reach out to us and want us to come do it there, and we even had two people in Washington who wanted to do it and give us a percentage of their profits for using our software. Basically do it under the exit strategy brand for Exit Strategy DC. The truth is it's not worth our time in other cities. A lot of New Yorkers think about this: where do I stand on the train? Not a lot of people in other cities necessarily think about it. I think in Washington it's less of a problem; the trains are shorter and people use them in a different way.

The sad truth is there's more of a market in selling a subway map than there is in this really cool data that we've collected. The original thinking behind the app was this is incredible data that nobody's bothered to collect because there's never been a reason to do it. And now the iPhone app is this brilliant micro-distribution solution, where we can literally charge 99 cents and put it in the hands of a million people. That was the original idea, and what we realized after our third day of being launched, and we were being outsold by iTrans on day 3, what was really depressing was that there is more of a market for the NYC subway map than there is for this cool data.

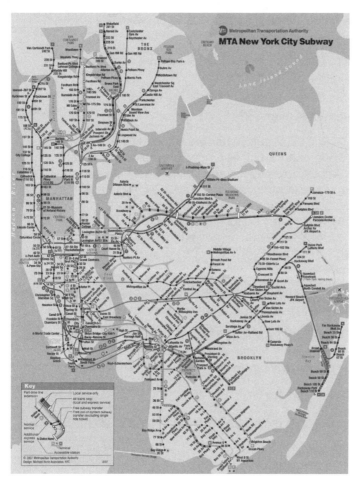

Figure 6–5. *For version 2.0, Wegener licensed the entirety of the Metropolitan Transit Authority's map collection, down to its hyper-local neighborhood drawings.*

How do you handle an update that's so major?

When the switch flips [on the new app] people overnight are going to see Exit Strategy develop into this beautiful butterfly. And hopefully they are going to be blown away, and go Tweet about it, and we'll try to do like kind of a second press launch. And the fact that we have this install-base that's getting it for free gives us word of mouth marketing powers, is my thinking. And once we get the update pushed to the store, we plan to raise the price.

Do you have an economic theory behind your pricing?

We did have plans to release a light version, that maybe only includes a single subway line so like just the 1 line data or something like that, to give people sort of a taste of what the app does and get them hooked on using it for one line. We just never really got around to it. We got distracted by other things, and then we started kind of working on version 2.0. It's going to be hard to make a light version of 2.0 unless we take what we have now and we make it Exit Strategy lite with just the exit data.

I hate the 99 cent price-point. I think it's really a ridiculous price-point. I see so much awesome software and it's really depressing that they're selling it for that pathetically low price. I knew we didn't want to do 99 cents, and we originally had thought we'd price this about $3.99 or $4.99 when we launched. And we talked to a whole bunch of friends, and interviewed everyone we knew with an iPhone. We kind of heard the same thing from everyone: I would never buy an app that costs more than $1.99. So we launched at $1.99, and we made the marketing round that the marketing was Less Than the Cost of Subway Ride! It got a chuckle out of the press, and almost every write put that in.

That was going to be our introductory price, and then we were going to raise it to $3.00 or $4.00, so that's what we did. After a week, we raised it to $3.00. The interesting thing was that there wasn't even a blip in the unit sales, they dropped by maybe 3 or 5% when we increased the price from two to three bucks. We should've done it [from the beginning] in retrospect; they were willing to pay $3.00 if they were willing to pay $2.

The barrier is once you get past, in my mind, $4.00. Anything over $4.00 is this premium price-point, where I'm not going to care if it's $8.00, $9.00, or $10.00. The most expensive thing I bought was a $10.00 app, the racing game from the Flight Control people.

I did try a $4.00 price-point for our current product, Exit Strategy 1.0, for a period, and we did see a revenue drop-off. So, I think there's always an ideal price-point, and it's fairly easy to test that. You just sort of increase or decrease the price until you figure out what that price-point is. So the really tough thing is launching a product like we did, because you don't have that knowledge, you don't have that market data, and you're completely going in the dark.

What we ultimately learned is that the people that care about where to stand on the subway, there's a lot of them, and they're really passionate about it, and they would pay $4.00 or even maybe $5.00. Or they couldn't care less and they wouldn't even pay a penny for it. So I think by trying to price it at this point where everyone could afford it and where everyone we thought would get it, which was our $2.00 launch price-point, in retrospect, that was a mistake.

How did you get attention for your app?

We very carefully made out our press strategy, and put out a media kit complete with images and videos. This whole cute story was sort of designed to be press-worthy. If I had paid someone on Craigslist $50.00 a day to go ride around, it would be a lot less interesting than the dedicated brother-sister team doing it. So, we definitely did everything with press in mind.

The New York Times broke the story with an exclusive. They had a copy of our app two weeks prior; I had gotten an introduction to someone at the CityRoom section. We had set up a connection at Thrillist, too, and it kind of took off from there. The day of launch, the Times came out with it 7:30 in the morning, at 10am I had a phone call from Wired magazine, then at 11am I had the New York Post on the phone. They all just sort of came to me. Putting my phone number on the press kit was one of the best things that I could've done.

You've chosen to go beyond the iPhone. Why?

We actually released this on four different platforms. We have it on iPhone, we have it on Blackberry, Android, and even as an eBook in Kindle. And that was really because of the design of it and the way we used images made it really easy to port.

The iPhone is 95% of the sales, but I wanted to have experience working across three different platforms.

In terms of porting it, it was really easy. My friend did it for us on Android in about 12 hours. Just because he was able to drag and drop the images in the database, and everything just transferred between platforms very easily because of that design.

What's the most important thing you learned making version 1.0?

There are two lessons. One is do your market research. I can't overstate that. The other lesson would be launch with the simplest product you can, the minimal viable product, or "MVP." Don't spend $50,000 in two years developing a product. Ours is incomplete; we don't even have the rest of NYC, and we get emails everyday from people that are angry that we don't have Avenue X on the Q line or something. Just get your product to market as quickly as you can, and improve it later, once you've discerned that there is a demand for your product.

Part IV

Creating a Beautiful App Without Falling Victim to Memory Issues—OpenGL, Skinning, Object Reuse, and Coding Efficiently

Building an app with beauty as well as brains can be an expensive process, so it's no wonder that the developers of the two apps in this section, Postage and Delicious Library, talk as much about their use of art as they do the deeply technical issues of memory management. But investing in aesthetics isn't enough. Good looks may wins impulse buyers, but it's an app's brains that keep those buyers using it long after they've come across competitors.

Postage is one of the friendliest single-purpose apps in the App Store, conceived originally with the developers' wives in mind: it lets you take a photo, choose a theme, and then send a rich email postcard. Delicious Library is cult favorite: a companion app for a desktop program that lets you catalog every item you own, and link some of them (books, movies, albums) to Amazon's database.

People buy Postage for very different reasons than Delicious Library, but the two apps are built on the same concept: if it's iPhone software, it needs to look damn good. Not only that, it needs to work damn good too. Want more damn goodness? Keep on reading.

Chapter 7

Postage

Developer Name: Chris Parrish and Brad Ellis
Development Company: Rogue Sheep
Tags: OpenGL ES; Art; Memory Management; Team Development
URL: http://postage.roguesheep.com/

This is the story of a band of engineers from a serious public software firm and their attempt to go solo and make serious software. What they ended up with: construction paper scraps on the floor, an ADA award, and one of the iPhone's most exquisite apps, Postage (shown in Figure 7–1).

Figure 7–1. *A postcard created in Postage, ready for in-app mailing.*

In 2002, five Adobe engineers from the Seattle office were culled together to work on a spinoff project, a scaled-down version of InDesign aimed at amateur publishers. The five would bond, code, and compile themselves into a working friendship. And when their project was killed in 2003, they'd jump ship in frustration, tumble into careers as coders-for-hire, and pop up in 2009 as the winners of an ADA for their picture-perfect postcard app for iPhone. This is the story of an unlikely bunch of aesthete engineers that calls itself RogueSheep.

There Were Sheep

The name isn't a purpose-built marketing tool or an age-old inside joke, according to Chris Parrish, one of the founding members of the flock. It's more of an analogy for how the company got started. "The name just kinda happened," says Parrish. "We went on a road trip to Oregon together. There were sheep, there was the Rogue River, and a microbrewery out there," he recalls. "It fits our character."

The outlier spirit is what drew the five members of the flock together in the first place, alone together as they were. "We never felt like we could ever do anything creative while we were at Adobe," says Parrish. "We felt removed from San Jose" [where Adobe is headquartered]. On a behemoth project like InDesign, Parrish says he and his cohorts would be among dozens of other engineers—up to 50 at one point, he remembers. "The creative expression and control you have is minimal; someone else is deciding what things should look like and feel like." It was only once he and his now-coworkers began the InDesign spinoff that they realized their chemistry. "We had similar sensibilities, and we had a really good time," he says. Another thing they had: new ideas. But in the Adobe hierarchy, new software concepts are bought, not incubated, Parrish says. They left the company as a group. "We thought, 'What can we do with this team?'"

The answer was they had no answer at all. "We kicked around a lot of ideas, and we talked about doing games," Parrish says. But each time the spaghetti hit the wall, nothing really stuck. Then one of the founders—the only one who has since left the team of the original five—came up with a proposal. His wife was doing her PhD dissertation at the University of Washington, and she was struggling with the software tools she was stuck using in the university labs. The group thought they had found their opportunity to build an elegant software solution. "Once someone had an idea that seemed remotely reasonable, we went with it," says Parrish.

The problem had to do with a painstaking research technique known as "gel electrophoresis," a process by which life science researchers analyze the nature of DNA and RNA samples. "The results of these experiments are these crude negative images," Parrish says. "A lot of the research is doing these experiments, and if you're going to publish your results, you have to label up these negatives. All that labeling was tedious, and they were doing all this diagramming and graphics work in PowerPoint, which was terrible," he says. They saw that the task needed graphical richness, but that it couldn't be static—it had to be alive with usability, and dynamic enough for revisions. "Interface concerns are high on the list of how we approach a problem," he says.

They set to work at RogueSheep's office in the Fremont district of Seattle. There, in the shadow of Seattle's unusual statue of V.I. Lenin, they began building a cross-platform solution with all the graphical potency they thought the problem warranted. Then they made a decision: they didn't want outside funding or interference. That meant picking up consulting and contract work to keep money coming in, but it also left almost no time for their own work. When they had time, the team played around with Apple's growing suite of apps. "We borrowed lots of ideas from iTunes and iPhoto," says Parrish. They were inspired. "Instead of just focusing on the labeling and output of these gel images, we totally retooled it," he says. They made the app into a kind of image notebook for researchers, complete with tagging, smart search, metadata, and exporting. But despite positive feedback from lab beta-testers, sales interest was tepid. After months of development, the project was tabled without so much as a name, but it had taught the team to pay acute attention to Mac UI. They ditched Windows and Linux and became full-time OS X developers.

Is This One of Them Internets?

Apple's 2008 WWDC was the group's deus ex machina. "Day to day, all of us run on Macs," says Parrish, "and only occasionally—and begrudgingly—do Windows software. The iPhone was a big thing for us. We were all excited." They showed up to San Francisco's Moscone Center in 2008, having heard about developers tinkering with the guts of the phone version of OS X long before the SDK was released. Once Apple announced their free iPhone developer kit, it opened the idea faucet. "We got the idea for Postage right there, at WWDC," says Parrish, at a company dinner. The first storyboard, created by the group's design guru, Brad Ellis, is shown in Figure 7–2. "It was a simpler time for the Postage project," he says.

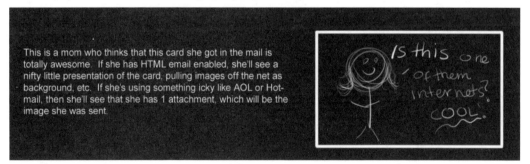

This is a mom who thinks that this card she got in the mail is totally awesome. If she has HTML email enabled, she'll see a nifty little presentation of the card, pulling images off the net as background, etc. If she's using something icky like AOL or Hotmail, then she'll see that she has 1 attachment, which will be the image she was sent.

Figure 7–2. *With a phone that can do rich HTML email, the possibilities for impressing peoples' moms became endless.*

The concept was simple: a rich, purpose-built app that would send electronic postcards based on photos taken with a user's iPhone. At the time of the ADAs in June 2009, Postage 1.1 did just that, and with aplomb. The app boasted 50 beautiful postcard templates, which users filled with their own photos they could pan, zoom, and rotate into any preferred orientation. To that photo, they could add one of several effects, such as a monochrome filter or sepia tone; they could also choose the color and font of the message text, and send the card to several recipients at once, all of which could be culled with a simple search from the iPhone's address book (the maximum number of recipients depends on how much of the phone's memory is available). The app is available in three languages—English, Dutch, and Italian. It won a fast audience with reviewers, both professional and otherwise. MacWorld called it a "perfect iPhone app," and users raved about the "exemplary" technical execution on the iTunes App Store.

As auspicious an app as Postage would be, the idea sat undeveloped for months after the team returned from WWDC 2008. Caught up in their contract work, RogueSheep simply didn't have enough manpower to do the fun stuff. It wasn't until February 2009 that they could peel off a couple of developers from paying gigs and begin in earnest. Luckily, Ellis had already begun spec'ing it out. Ellis' second storyboard is show in Figure 7–3.

Figure 7–3. *A more detailed Postage storyboard, this version drawn without anyone's mom.*

Even so, they were behind: the SDK had already been out for the better part of the year. "All our peers had figured [the App Store] out a year ago," says Ellis. "We were late to the game." But while the PR blitz around the iPhone had begun to wane, Ellis' excitement had only begun to ramp up. "What I enjoyed was looking at the UI stuff," he says. "With the iPhone [I] got to totally start over, and put aside all that other knowledge I had been accumulating. You just get to start fresh."

He started a torrent of downloading—by his own account, "all the free apps" in the iTunes store. "I've checked out all of them," he repeats. The potential for a simple, beautiful, functional app had a powerful allure, but not a lot of fiscal incentive. "The economics of the App Store had really changed" since the early days of $100,000 overnight sales, recalls Parrish. "We didn't know what was possible. We just knew that it would be worth doing just to get leads for other jobs."

Coding for Fun

What the iPhone platform lacked in business incentives, it had in entertainment. "I haven't had that much fun programming since I was a kid," says Parrish. There was almost no learning curve switching between Mac and iPhone development, he recalls, making the challenge purely creative and only minimally technical. Fueling the innovation were dozens of other excellent iPhone apps that the RogueSheep guys say inspired them to keep their expectations for their own work high. "Classics is a great example that makes you reach for a higher bar," Parrish says of the intricate iPhone book reader built by Andrew Kazmierski, which had received over 3,000 four- and five-star ratings in the iTunes store as of WWDC 2009. Another source of inspiration is developer Will Shipley's iPhone version of Delicious Library 2, the catalog-everything-you-own software that recognizes CDs and books by viewing them through your Mac's iSight camera. "We hung out with him a lot [while developing Postage]," says Ellis. The list of plaudits doesn't stop there: the RogueSheep guys also say they marvel at the brilliance of NewsGator's NetNewsWire client for iPhone, and the Twinkle Twitter client by prolific game maker Tapulous, creator of the TapTap line of iPhone games.

Yet even with so many adroit developers building for the iPhone, Parrish says, his team found they drew even more inspiration from elsewhere. "In a lot of ways, we were more inspired by Mac apps, thinking we wanted to translate that kind of experience to the iPhone," he says. And when it came to those, well, there was really one company that epitomized brilliance. "All of us strive to think: what would Apple do? Some of the native apps on the iPhone are what we're really trying to match with our own interface, and our presentation to the user." But Ellis, ever the paper-and-glue throwback, credits actual postcards for the beauty he built into Postage. "I wanted it to be like a physical postcard, and I've been trying to hammer that idea home from day one," he says. "It's what I've picked up from my art background."

Although they might not share muses, the entire team at RogueSheep seems united under an umbrella principle that is palpable in Postage: zero learning curve usability. "This was built for our wives," Parrish says. "We wanted them to be able to use the app without ever having to hesitate or get confused." Ellis chimes in: "In fact, a wife that doesn't even have an iPhone should be able to pick up someone's iPhone and be able to use it." The key to usability, the RogueSheep engineers believe, is concise, narrow focus, something that they believe Apple has mastered. "It's not necessarily having every option, but having the right options, so people don't have to put in a lot of effort to generate something that's beautiful," Parrish says. "That's one of the great things about the Apple applications for the desktop," he says. "Look at Numbers; you can create beautiful spreadsheets with very minimal effort. You don't have every option that Excel has, but it has most of what most people need, and the end result is just beautiful. That's a big motivating factor."

While the challenge of building Postage wasn't in the method—the RogueSheep engineers were all Mac-happy Objective C developers to begin with—it presented the bright, obsessive team with dozens of new ways to streamline the way it worked. While their workspace is in flux due to an office overhaul, the company's first since its founding, the stockpile of tools in its arsenal is ever-growing. There are plenty of the trademark silver Apple towers, they say, but not the ones you expect; only Ellis has a Mac Pro. "All our desktops are G5s that we've had forever," says Parrish. "We really haven't had the need for the brand new eight-core Mac Pro's. I'm a developer—I'm supposed to need the biggest, baddest machine," he says quizzically, "but the G5s are at a sweet spot where they're still quite usable. I spend more time thinking about what I'm going to do than waiting for it to do something." With Snow Leopard on the verge of release, he concedes, the team might have to make a capital investment. "We may have to replace them," he says a little glumly.

The G5s have help: an array of 15-inch MacBook Pros and a few dual-monitor setups. "I can't get enough screen space," says Parrish. "I have two monitors, and Spaces, plus the laptop." Ellis, as the resident creative, has a tablet-centric setup and "matching pen cups for different color pens." Unlike the other developers, Ellis has spent much of his Postage project time working on video and still mockups. "All the animation for Postage has been done in Motion beforehand," he says, and iterations he created in Photoshop were often dozens of layers deep, containing smart objects that themselves contained dozens of layers. "Before we started coding it at all, I had made what each screen looked like in a big Photoshop document," says Ellis. "This document ended up housing every asset, so I could look at the whole screen while I was tweaking my pixels." (See Figure 7–4, a .psd mockup.)

Figure 7–4. *A Photoshop mockup featuring Ellis' two roommates. "Little differences here and there," Ellis says, "but generally we knew exactly what the application was going to look like before we even started."*

To allow the team to keep tabs on his progress, Ellis used a tool called LiveView. Written by an industrial design firm in Palo Alto called Ideo, it's a screen-casting app for both desktop and iPhone. The desktop iteration, ScreenCaster, presents a small, iPhone-shaped bezel on the screen of your Mac. Drag the bezel around your screen, and whatever's inside will appear magically on any iPhone within your LAN that is running LiveView for iPhone. "Everyone could pipe in and see my progress," says Ellis. "It was kinda fun."

Longtime Mac developers, the RogueSheep crew remembers the days when Apple's own dev kit wasn't so hot. "Xcode has really matured a lot," Parrish says, describing the way it caught up to—then overtook—Microsoft's tools for Windows developers with its killer feature set. "It's so awesome to see Apple having money coming in, and on this growth path," he says, "because its teams are chartering new territory now. Ten was always a superior platform, but Project Builder was a little dated," he says of Xcode's predecessor. "The features are there. I'd be lost without Xcode now." Even when they have to develop for Windows, Parrish says, some members of the team often write the rough draft of a program in Apple's IDE, putting it into Visual Studio only when they must.

The Circling Shark

While many iPhone developers run light apps that never come close to exceeding the iPhone's 64MB allotted memory for apps—which is effectively only 20-30MB in practice, say the RogueSheep engineers—the development of Postage relied unusually on Apple's tools to optimize and reign in memory management. "Without Shark and Instruments, we couldn't have gotten Postage working. It would have been so hard to figure out why it was crashing [in early versions]," says Parrish. The problem, he adds, is that all of Ellis' intricate images and textures hog memory. "We were running into problems at the 'sent' screen. The app would be hitting the memory max, and then in the background the phone goes to check for mail, blowing us over the limit," he says. While he concedes that the task of keeping Postage within Apple's memory guidelines is easier now, thanks to improvements in iPhone OS 3.0 and OpenGL 2.0 ES, the original development process meant keeping a squeaky-clean leak profile. And it wasn't just memory leaks that almost killed the app, says Parrish, but restrictions of the iPhone's framework itself. "We had to make tradeoffs between performance and memory," Parrish admits. One example: at first the team wanted to keep lots of elements at the ready to ensure quick load times, but memory economy dictated they resort to lazy loading. Then Ellis wanted to use a torn-edge look for the perimeter of the templates, but it ballooned the file sizes of some assets. "That's one of our strong suits," says Ellis, of memory management. "Originally [Postage] was crashing after sending four postcards, and Chris said, 'No, dammit, we're going to be able to send as many postcards in a row as we need to.'"

"You have to go past the regular usage scenarios to get to what you expect to be stable," Parrish adds. Cutting down the graphical quality of the app's assets was never an option, the team agrees. "If your app has 200 frames and is under 10MB, then I think you're doing it wrong," says Ellis.

The engineers still feared their app might get into a cycle of crashing on launch because of bad persistent data. "We had seen this happen to a number of developers, and the end result was not pretty," says Parrish. Because of Apple's long wait times for app update approval, users could be left for weeks with non-functioning apps whose only remedy was deletion and a fresh install—a pretty "violent" solution, as Parrish says.

The team decided to write a little flag into the app's NSUserDefaults when the application starts. If the app crashed on startup more than once, the flag would activate and blow away that persistent data after the next crash. "Ultimately you'd like to just never have a bug with your saved data," Parrish says. "The reality is, it's going to happen to you at some point. This technique can at least manage the user experience to something more reasonable on a platform like the iPhone, where the data storage is opaque to the user and it's not trivial for them to take an action to fix the problem themselves."

Describing the flag, he says: "We clear it when the application quits normally. In the event of an abnormal quit, the flag is not cleared. We note the state of this flag at startup; if it's the second time the flag is not cleared, we take action to remove all the saved data and start with a clean slate."

If your app pushes the limits of the iPhone, it may pay to implement boolean expressions like those in Postage. The following are some of the relevant API calls.

```
RSCrashDetector class :

- (void) appStarting
{
NSUserDefaults* defaults = [NSUserDefaults standardUserDefaults];
BOOL crashedOnce = [defaults boolForKey: kCrashDetectorAppLaunchedKey];
BOOL crashedTwice = [defaults boolForKey: kCrashDetectorAppLaunchedAfterCrashKey];

[defaults setBool: YES forKey: kCrashDetectorAppLaunchedKey];
[defaults setBool: crashedOnce forKey: kCrashDetectorAppLaunchedAfterCrashKey];
[defaults synchronize];

crashedTwice_ = crashedTwice;
}


- (void) appTerminating
{
NSUserDefaults* defaults = [NSUserDefaults standardUserDefaults];
[defaults setBool: NO forKey: kCrashDetectorAppLaunchedKey];
[defaults setBool: NO forKey: kCrashDetectorAppLaunchedAfterCrashKey];
}

In the Application Delegate :

- (void)applicationDidFinishLaunching:(UIApplication *)application
{
...

RSCrashDetector* detector = [RSCrashDetector crashDetector];
[detector appStarting];
// Initialization stuff

...

if ( detector.crashedTwice )
{
[[RSPostcard sharedPostcard] clearState];
}
}

- (void)applicationWillTerminate:(UIApplication *)application
{
// Save data if appropriate
...

RSCrashDetector* detector = [RSCrashDetector crashDetector];
[detector appTerminating];
}
```

As fickle as the iPhone platform can feel, Parrish says that its tight-fitting restrictions belie the creativity it inspires. "Everyone wants garbage collection [for iPhone], but we all know that would make the phone terribly slow," he says. "But to those of us who would be called old school, it's like going back to the Apple II. It's this restricted environment.

We're used to 10 gigs of RAM and unlimited power," he says, "but if you're trying to develop an app that's sophisticated like Postage, the memory management is nostalgic. Sometimes limitations make you produce your best stuff." Ellis says he likes that it puts new developers and old alike on equal footing in the race for new ideas. "We're given a clean slate as user interface and experience designers," he says, "and it's time to go back to the core ideas that computers were founded upon and redefine everything so it makes sense in our new world. I don't have a tremendous amount of experience designing for the iPhone, but nobody does, which actually makes me right with the rest of the crowd out of the gate."

Homegrown Design

To say that RogueSheep produced its "best stuff," as Parrish calls it, doesn't quite do justice to the massive graphical effort that went into Postage's postcard templates. "Everything in these templates is me-generated," Ellis says. And he's not simply talking about the interface, though all the buttons and nav designs are his, too. "The textures, the components ... lots of them are made from physical objects, all scanned and set up," he says. The 50 templates that come with each copy of Postage are full of mementos. "A photo of a flower I brought in, or a paper I made when I was nine in class that I've been holding onto because I'm a pack-rat," Ellis says. Others contributed, too. "Chris' wife Liz took their kids down to the beach and got shells; Chris' son Aiden has one of his shells in a template in the travel category," he adds. "Everything in the Cutouts category was all cut from large sheets of construction paper by Liz and scanned into the computer." One of the creative challenges the templates presented was how to give users a lot of options, but still maintain a common visual language throughout. "The templates are already a scattershot of different styles and flavors. I constantly fought an internal battle over how different each template looked from one another," says Ellis. "There are so many different styles all packaged together." (Figure 7–5 shows the construction paper elements of the dinosaur theme. Figure 7–6 shows the finished product.)

The team was careful to organize all the app's graphical elements in a way that would be conducive to easy, fluid user interaction. "We made the decision early on to have the templates and backgrounds be different assets," Ellis explains. "It makes it easier to put your photo into fun shapes, like this dinosaur mouth. It also lets us animate the card without moving the background on the iPhone." The distinction is part of what Ellis says is "underlying concept" of Postage: "You're working on a card, and the card should be separate from the background."

Figure 7–5. *The actual paper cutouts made and scanned by Parrish's wife for the "dinosaur" template.*

Figure 7–6. *The finished template. "Everything is from us, by us, and made with love," Ellis says.*

For all the praise among developers and designers for Apple's UI kit—the standardized controls, the carefully crafted buttons—what truly sets Postage apart is how its bevy of homemade stuff has all been buffed and polished to be consonant with the Apple aesthetic. That was part of the goal, according to Ellis, who says that his greatest takeaway from Postage, which his first major development project, was "learning how to make things that look like Apple" but that underneath are the weird, wild products of his own brain.

Ellis, who is 23 and studied visual arts at the nearby University of Washington, says, "I really enjoy real objects, and I try to infuse that in my design stuff." In school he took sculpture and metal work, and didn't bother with computer art classes after having mastered Photoshop as a high-schooler. "I bring in a lot more of my physical art concepts than traditional computer paradigms," he says. "Postage is about working on a card, it's not about filling out text boxes. While we were working out the animations between each screen, I had a set of props in the office that were the different elements of the interface." That way, he says, "I could explain to everyone the layering and the moving of everything, as it exists in a physical space."

While the RogueSheep team agrees that Apple is a paradigm house of good design, much of the distinction they achieved with Postage came from avoiding the iPhone's general user logic and replacing it with something purpose-built. "We really thought about Postage from the ground up, tangential to the existing iPhone interfaces," says Ellis. "What's the right thing for the user?" The answer to that question was sometimes to fall back on iPhone controls and looks, he says, "but it's important to always have the flexibility to step back and say 'this is going to be different because it's the right answer.'"

Despite the considerable effort it takes to make each template—at most Ellis says he could crank out six a day—there were still a lot that didn't make it into Postage. (Figure 7–7 shows just how much production was required to keep the templates looking consistent.)

"We had to throw some away," Ellis says, mournfully. In hindsight, some of the sacrifices he made—especially those cut in the name of App Store approval—weren't all necessary. As Parrish recounts: "The weekend we were going to put [Postage] in the app store, I came across something online that said that people who made apps with pictures that look like Polaroids got rejected for copyright infringement. At the last minute we yanked those templates." Then he came upon other Polaroid copycat apps soon thereafter, confused. (Figure 7–8, the original icon for Postage, which was scrapped because of its use of Polaroid-like photos.)

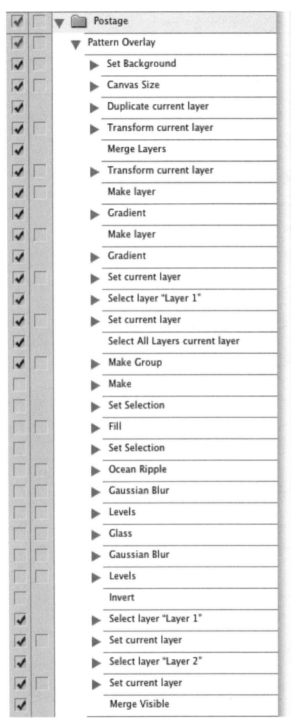

Figure 7–7. *A complex Photoshop action that Ellis applied to each background tile mockup before inserting it into Postage.*

Figure 7–8. *The first Postage icon, which included a Polaroid-like photo. They remade the icon for fear of App Store rejection.*

The discarded template will be re-added to the next Postage update, the engineers say, which will be free. "In the desktop world, you wouldn't be getting new templates free," says Ellis, "you'd get what you buy. But everyone on the reviews is talking about what's coming next—everyone expects [free] updates," he says.

Like other developers, RogueSheep has plenty of antipathy for the app approval process, but theirs is particularly hard earned: using analytics, they were able to see that Apple's reviewer performed less than a half an hour of testing on their app before rejecting it during the first Postage submission.

"That black hole sucks," says Parrish of the approval machine. "When we first submitted, you couldn't really do an image attachment in Mail 2.0 using a built-in image. So we planned to build a web service that would mail the picture: our app would connect to that web server to send the picture. In the process, before we got into the nitty-gritty of the app, a friend of ours that now works at Apple released an SMTP client that was open source. So we made the decision that we could have it send through our server, so the user wouldn't have to enter in any kind of configuration to make it work. SMPT is a well-known protocol, and it should scale, and it should mean less work for us on the back end. The caveat to that is—which we knew, but which we didn't think would be a problem—that a lot of corporate networks will block SMTP traffic that isn't from their own servers; any other attempt to send email through any other server is blocked for security reasons."

That's exactly what happened at Apple. The reviewer's postcard failed to send, earning them a rejection. "But the reviewer was only ever connected to the WiFi network," Parrish says. "We have analytics in the app that showed the app was only run once. We had the expectation that the people reviewing it would have a little more knowledge," he says. "It seemed absurd that you would test an application for the store and never run it on the cellular network." After almost a year of brainstorming, 30 to 35 weeks of labor, months of sticking half their team on the app full time, and 10 days of waiting, they were crestfallen. "The first time we were rejected, I felt like, 'No more iPhone apps!'" says Ellis. "It felt like you didn't get into college."

But being a pro developer has its perks. The RogueSheep guys were able to open a case with friends at Apple's Developer Support, even though Apple doesn't traditionally allow its support network to extend to the app approval process. By registering the issue, the team avoided having to reengineer the whole back end mailer for Postage.

"Most of us who are trying to make a business out of this are fine with rules, and fine with Apple dictating those rules," says Parrish. "But it's not like you have a case history [with app approval], or any consistency." In fact, the engineers say, it was difficult to take even educated guesses at how to best suit the content of their app to a passing grade, because Apple will frequently reject an element of an app that was approved in an earlier version. "It's complete happenstance," says Parrish. For most developers, Apple's caprice will be discouraging, but happenstance works both ways. Tweak, re-tweak, and submit again; with a different reviewer, your app is bound to find justice and get in the store.

Building On Postage

The iPhone has also proven itself to be creative catnip. With desktop development, the possibility for invention is so limitless that it's almost enervating. It's also been well-worn in the 22 years since NeXT licensed Objective C from a software company called Stepstone. But the iPhone means a new user experience for a new kind of computer, something that begets totally new concepts, as well as adaptations of old ones. "Developers have seen their imaginations run riot with ideas for software that might have been too small for the Mac, but fit the iPhone just right," says Parrish. RogueSheep is no different. "We have many whiteboards here, full of growing lists of apps," he says. "It's hard to pick which one to do." The team says they find the new ability to work with video on the 3GS compelling, but they say the SDK hasn't quite caught up with the hardware. "Do we build all the scaffolding we'd need to do cool things with video, or wait and see if Apple does it?" Parrish says. "We're trying to read the tea leaves, so we've been bugging the Apple offices to try to figure out what their plan is." Whatever they decide to build, there's a good chance that no one has ever built it before. If there's ever been a creative credential that gets engineers excited, it's that one. (Other developers don't wait around for Apple; Intermap, also featured in Chapter 5 of this book, decided to build their own mapping framework for their ADA-winning app, AccuTerra.)

By the time RogueSheep gets back to building its own pet iPhone apps, the development landscape may have changed. Tools like WebApp.net are allowing developers with no C programming experience to mimic the iPhone GUI on their web sites, eschewing any need to build a native app. The kit provides items based on JavaScript and CSS, works with server-side technologies like PHP, ASP, and ASP.NET, and because all a user has to do to access the app is bookmark the purpose-built site, it also obviates Apple's approval process. Other programs like NimbleKit by VolnaTech give you desktop software that allows you to build a native iPhone app using popular web languages. NimbleKit works by providing its own API on top of Cocoa touch, allowing users to build apps from a HTML templates with embedded JavaScript, and then submit them to the App Store.

Web-language evangelists see this kind of tool as the ultimate democratizing force, and chide Apple for relying on programming languages that aren't universal. Though Objective C is a strict superset of C, meaning that any snippet of a C language you include will be valid, proponents of the web-as-standard movement (which count notables like Jon von Tetzchner, founder and CEO of Opera, among their ranks) say that the only way to move forward in a world of multiple devices and platforms is to count on JavaScript and HTML 5 as lingua franca. The RogueSheep engineers disagree. "The barrier to entry is clearly not Objective C and Cocoa," says Parrish, noting that as of this writing, there are nearly 100,000 apps in the App Store. Too much has been made of devices like the Palm Pre, whose JavaScript-based webOS are touted as more accessible, he says. "I've almost gotten to the point where I almost think that's a ridiculous thing to say. All these people managed to learn Objective C to put an app in the App Store. There's a learning curve to do it right, but that's true of everything. You have to take your time to understand your frameworks."

So it will go for RogueSheep, eager to see what Apple will unlock next and what kind of revenue and beauty will be at the other side. They won't need much patience for that, says Ellis. "Everything is changing so quickly, it'll be interesting to see where we are a year from now. I assume all of next year's ADA winners will blow us out of the water."

Chapter 8

Q&A: Delicious Library

Developer Name: Wil Shipley
Development Company: Delicious Monster
Tags: Client App; Visual Design; Memory Management; Efficient Code
URL: http://delicious-monster.com/

What the iPhone lacks in size it does not have to lack in luster. Delicious Library, the companion app to the Mac desktop program Delicious Library 2, allows a user to sync his Mac's database of scanned books, movies, albums, and other sundries via iPhone, complete with Amazon information, covers, summaries, reviews, and other data. (See Figure 8–1.) It's a model iPhone client for the desktop version: quick to update its database, easy to navigate, beautiful to behold and massively scalable.

Figure 8–1. *Library for iPhone is a model client app, and shares aesthetics with its desktop version.*

Delicious Library for iPhone was built by Wil Shipley and two outside UI designers. Shipley is the founder and sole engineer of his company, Delicious Monster, and also an original co-founder of the Omni Group. Over the course of his career, he has won seven ADAs, one for the desktop version of Delicious Library in 2005. You can find his popular Pimp My Code blogging series at his personal site, http://wilshipley.com.

This app is interesting not only in its execution, but also as a reminder that the rules of this platform have yet to be wholly defined. In July 2009, the Delicious Library for iPhone was removed from the App Store due to a violation of Amazon's API terms, which dictate that Amazon content cannot be used in mobile applications.[1] When Shipley protested, Amazon didn't provide a reason for its policy; should it change, we'll again see Library in the App Store. Until then, this app will have to be appreciated post-mortem.

What's behind the theming?

It was a pain to get that wood paneling working, because we wanted to use standard objects, just in terms of programming. But the iPhone doesn't have a super-fast processor, so we were constantly [making] a trade-off between animation and graphic performance, to have it actually be responsive. Responsiveness is as important to the feel of an app as the graphical interface is. You end up spending a lot of time trying to get everything both fast and beautiful, which is really not fun.

I actually spent six months on this app, which is a pretty long time. It was a read-only app, but I really sweated all the details. The foundation of it was, it was supposed to be part one of a three-part app, where I was upgrading it to have more functionality. But that's obviously on hold.

Your plan was to get it looking right first and foremost?

Yes. What most [Delicious Library users] said was, "We want an iPhone app." I was like, wait: there are a lot of issues, more than you might think. So I started [with aesthetics].

One of the things we wanted to do was go a little beyond flat table views, although I didn't want to get too fancy. I wanted to keep it very conceptually simple, and also I wanted to keep it simple, programming-wise, because every time you add any animation, it's just a ton of programming work.

There's an app called Pantscast, which is really funny app—it's one of these farting apps, for putting fart sounds into podcasts. But what's funny about it is that it's so well done—just incredibly polished. It's an absolute work of art. When you switch from the podcast, it kind of slides from side to side, like the old first version of AppleTV. You

---

[1] http://www.delicious-monster.com/downloads/Delicious%20Library%202/
DeliciousLibraryVersionTwo.html

slide, slide, slide, and the thing sort of swooshes in and swishes out, and it looks just fantastic. [Scrolling through podcasts in Pantscast, Figure 8–2.]

My artists were pitching me on that as well, like, "Let's add it to when you switch between books, animate and animate out, resize…," and I'm like, "No, No, No! We're going to use the standard scroll view, and it's going to scroll side to side."

Figure 8–2. *Pantscast's elegance belies its fart noises. "It's an absolute work of art," says Shipley.*

Why were you so dead-set against animation?

From Delicious Library, I learned that animations can take so long to get feeling right, that if you do them in a half-ass way, they just feel horrible. It also complicates programming amazingly, because everything we program right now, where we say, "Hey do this," then it's done. When you animate, you sort of say, "Hey start doing this," and then you're in weird in-between state, and you have to start handling that. You're not showing Card A, and you're not showing Card B, you're showing something in-between. That gets really tricky. It's a lot of extra code, and I don't want to spend an extra three months doing animation.

So skinning was the healthy medium?

Yeah, I was really proud of what we did. When you drill all the way down to books or CDs, and you flip between them, I'm particularly proud of the flipping. I showed it to Apple, and they were, at the time, really impressed—but this was before the new frameworks had come out. It was really tricky to do scrolling left and right and up and down at the same view, and they really liked how mine felt. I ended up sending them the sample code to do that. Under the 3.0 framework, there's like a single check mark you had to do, but in 1.0 and 2.0, it was a little bit harder.

But regardless of [3.0], I was also proud of just the feel of speed—that you could switch between items, when you're drilling all the way down to CDs, and you swipe your fingers to see another CD—it's all really fast. It was a real trick and it was fun, and then the Palm Pre came out, and we started using that same sort of metaphor with the UI, and I felt really good about it. We had semi-anticipated it on the app. (Figure 8–3 shows Delicious Library's card system at work.)

Figure 8–3. *Library's "card" system harkens back to the Palm Pre.*

How did you achieve that speed?

There were a bunch of different speed-ups to be done. One thing was being very careful to manage when I actually draw the new cards, so I don't draw them in the middle of the animations: I try really hard to do all the other [processing] after the animations are done, or before the animation starts. If you're looking at an item, I'll draw on an item from the left or right of it, so if you switch, it will just flick a random bitmap on the screen, without having to render it, because it turns out during scrolling it's really expensive to do almost anything. Allocating memory during scrolling, even the tiniest bit of memory, is phenomenally better. So I did process of elimination, where I made sure these objects are reused and these objects are pre-allocated, all these little tricks. You can do a bunch of different things, it's just all about allocating memory. I had no idea, at first: that's just some real weird quirk of the software, that allocating is way more expensive than anything else. If you allocate two bytes, you're waiting forever.

I made sure my memory [usage] just never grew above 5MB, ever, and that was a really neat thing, because this is an app where I was thinking of collections of 10,000 books and their high-res covers—that's a huge database. There's no one out there that has 10,000 contexts, there's almost nothing on the phone 10,000 of anything, except iTunes, and maybe the photo browser. Because I used a real database, it was very smooth. It was a really fun thing to program; it was like programming the Apple II.

How does that database work?

It was pretty interesting to solve that problem. Right now the [desktop] app just bundles up a special version of the database, and ships the whole database off to the iPhone, and there's some really great advantages to that. It was really cool cause I didn't know I could do that, and then I went to a tech talk with the guy who wrote SQLite 3, and he explained that SQLite can go from any device to any other device and will always be compatible with the data file, and that suddenly made everything a lot easier. I figured, I'll just take my existing Core data database, sort it out to SQLite.

What I do on the Mac side is I create another Core database, because at the time, there was no Core data on the iPhone. I thought it would probably come, so I wanted to be compatible. So what I do is instead of having to write my own SQL on the Mac side, I just wrote out a second Core data database which has only the fields and information that you're going to be interested in on the iPhone, like much smaller versions of the pictures—stuff like that.

Then I just manually compressed and copied the raw binary across to the iPhone, and it ended up being surprisingly fast when I got the networking cleaned up.

That's a lot of data, isn't it?

Yeah, it's really surprising how fast the iPhone can squirt data across the wireless. I was actually stunned at the transfer rate. I felt really good: it was squirting across this 30MB file, which the receiving processor sits there and collects into memory, and writes out to disk before reading the file back from disk. It then compresses, and then writes the uncompressed one back to disk.

I did it this way because it was very fast way to do it on the Mac. But this was before I knew anything about the iPhone's memory. Then I started getting crashes the second or third time I'd sync, and I finally found out these limits—you can't read a 30MB file into memory, you'll crash and blow up the RAM. It's funny cause that shouldn't even have worked once.

You didn't, um, RTFM?

I went back and looked around, and it's not just in the common documentation. Not anywhere. There's nowhere in the documentation that you'll read these magic 5MB and

20MB numbers. They're trying to protect themselves against the future, but it's total bullshit, because then I have no clue. What am I working with? Is it gigabytes? They don't even publish how much physical RAM you have, much less how much you can use. Worse, there's no system call to get it. Most of the stuff they've written is to play up the iPhone, not call out its limitations. [Apple] is like, "Yeah we have a real virtual memory system," and I'm like, "Oh, real virtual memory, then it won't ever crash?"

Then finally they're like, "Oh we have a real virtual memory system, but we don't have demand paging for RAM allocation." And I'm saying, "What!?" That's when I realized that I had written this program as if I were writing on a big computer when I really should have been thinking of it as an embedded device.

I had to go back and rewrite it to graph 5 bytes off the network, and immediately run this through the SQL uncompressor, and then, immediately write that to disk, and then flush that memory and do it again. And so it never, so it went from using 60MB to transfer a 30MB database to using 10k, and it got a little faster in the process. It was a good win. But when you're switching from the Mac to this device, you really have to remember, "Oh I just can't just magically map in a 30MB file."

Did you consider making the app standalone?

I seriously considered it, and there were people that were trying to talk me into it. Maybe if I got [barcode] scanning to work well, I would've thought about it more. There are some apps that are pretty valid as standalones on the iPhone.

Here's the thing: I really think the future is gonna be about families of apps, where you have the same data on different devices, and you just have different capabilities on every device. I just don't see someone wanting to spend a lot of time on their little iPhone, editing their particular library—but I could be wrong about that. I'm planning a very functional desktop app for my next project, with hopefully an iPhone or tablet app that is a viewer, but a "viewer-plus." It won't be just static, but a viewer you can really interact with.

I definitely knew what I didn't want to do. There are a lot of apps out there that are, you know, really half-assed. Like, there's this Lonely Planet guide out in which they just kind of dumped a flat list of information into an app as quickly as possible. That really stinks.

I also have mixed feelings about Apple's remote app for their iTunes, which I use all the time and think is pretty damn cool. But honestly the flow of it is a little bizarre, so I get lost a lot in it, and if I'm getting lost, it seems like other people would also get lost. So I kept that in mind.

Were you looking to imitate the desktop experience?

I wanted something where you could instantly dive into it if you knew the desktop. So we wanted to keep the hierarchies intact, but the way you switch between the items in detail view is new, even though it still feels kind of like the desktop. [Delicious Library 2, pictured in Figure 8–4.]

I knew from the beginning that I didn't just want to do what a lot of people would do, which is to just make a miniature version of Delicious Library: have nine books on the screen, in a three-by-three matrix. I knew from the beginning that just wasn't going to cut it, it's just not enough information for the screen. I always thought that maybe we'd go back to that—that at some point, if you turned the phone sideways it would switch to shelf view, or if you turned it back it would switch to the table view. But obviously they killed my app before I got a chance to do it.

Figure 8–5. *Delicious Library 2's desktop interface. "I didn't just want to do what a lot of people would do, which is to just do a miniature version of Delicious Library," says Shipley.*

Delicious Library overlaps a little with iTunes. How did you deal with that paradigm?

I didn't really want to mimic it at all. I don't actually use my iPhone as an iPod, so honestly, I don't even really know how their iPod app works. It's really funny: for a while I kept thinking, this is really cool, when I did this app. Then I realized Apple's actually done much the same thing for their app in the iPod.

When I first did the album view in Delicious Library 2, I was really happy with that look, and then iTunes [for Mac] came out and mimicked it, but they never tried to go quite as far for it. They don't have the backgrounds, they are not trying to make it quite as rich. They're not trying to be the same thing, and I think that's sort of respectable.

In sort of the same way, I almost put in iTunes syncing through Delicious Library 2 with the iPhone, but then I realized that this is different. People like me don't have all their music on their iPhones, but they still love it to store all of their albums there. It's a very chic way to see if you own something or not, because you don't store the actual thing on the device.

Other challenges we haven't talked about?

Absolutely. In just re-skinning the widgets, the whole toolkit is so new that half of those functions, those message calls, have never been called by man. They're just bizarre. They're telling you that you can do this, but no one has ever done it. So at the time that I did my table view, no one had done a table view with a repeating text or background. There was just a bunch of calls that hadn't been called, and didn't really work the way you want them to, or would think they would. It's truly all-new, and new stuff keeps showing up.

What's interesting is that they always err on the side of not giving you enough tools instead of giving you too many. There was just a bunch of stuff in 2.0 like that. They gave you buttons, but they're like, "If you'd like to draw buttons, it will be a white button with black border and black text, and that's it, that's the only kind of button we have." Of course, this kind of button appears nowhere in Apple's apps, so this is total bullshit. They use these beautiful app buttons, and give us absolutely no way to draw them ourselves, without completely doing it from scratch, or completely reinventing the whole button. "Here this is your toolkit, and it looks like ass, and here's our toolkit and it looks great."

Specifically, they gave us absolutely no way to do primary shines or primitive washes or colors or anything. If you're making a button toolkit, you really should say, "Here's our standard button shine," and you could call it whatever, and you'd get the shine, and you're good to go. That's obvious.

Did you bring this up to engineers at Apple?

Yeah, but they're always like, "Blah blah blah, we didn't have enough time."

What would you tell someone starting app tomorrow?

The memory thing is the biggest. It's just absolutely the biggest. It's not about the processor with this thing; it's about the memory. And that's a big lesson. In the Apple IIE it was about the processor first, and the memory second. So this is a real switch for me to be like, wow, when it's not encumbered by stuff, the iPhone is a surprisingly fast little guy. And so it's really all about finding ways to not allocate memory repeatedly; that is, to reuse objects again and again and again. That's just something you'd never do on a Mac. It doesn't help your performance, and it kind of can hurt it in a lot of cases, so it's something I was trained out of doing. I used to do it in the old days, back in 1993 and 1994, but not since. So it's weird to go back to that.

Another thing was I learned was to use tricks to allocate blocks of things when the user is idle. You want to pre-compute some stuff, when the user is just staring at you, so that you can have it right there ready.

The third thing is just making sure that any operation you do, you do it in tiny little chunks. Don't download an entire file and then save it like you would on the Mac, though that's still pretty dumb on the Mac, honestly. And if you're processing something, you should load in a couple bytes, and process them and squirt them out.

[In the following example, Shipley shares his way of reusing UI text views. "I have this in my superclass for my data-bearing objects," he says. "Note that it's up to the implementer to write the clearProperties method to clean up the object when it's getting recycled or freed — this method essentially replaces 'dealloc'."

To use, just call +newInstance. Note that this code doesn't return an auto-released object, since auto-releasing on the iPhone isn't always optimal.]

```
static NSMutableDictionary *classesToReusableInstanceArrays = nil;

#pragma mark NSObject

- (void)release;
{
    if (self.retainCount > 1)
        return [super release];

    if (!classesToReusableInstanceArrays)
        classesToReusableInstanceArrays = [[NSMutableDictionary alloc] init];

    NSMutableArray *reusableInstanceArray = [classesToReusableInstanceArrays
objectForKey:[self class]];
    if (!reusableInstanceArray) {
        reusableInstanceArray = [[NSMutableArray alloc] init];
        [classesToReusableInstanceArrays setObject:reusableInstanceArray forKey:[self
class]];
        [reusableInstanceArray release];
    }

    [self clearProperties];
    [reusableInstanceArray addObject:self];
    [self release];
}

- (void)dealloc;
{
    [self clearProperties];
    [super dealloc];
}


#pragma mark API

+ (id)newInstance;
{
    NSMutableArray *reusableInstanceArray = [classesToReusableInstanceArrays
objectForKey:[self class]];
    id newInstance = [reusableInstanceArray lastObject];
    if (newInstance) {
        [newInstance retain];
        [reusableInstanceArray removeLastObject];
```

```
        return newInstance;
    }
    return [[self alloc] init];
}

- (void)clearProperties;
{
    self.foo = nil;
    self.bar = nil;
}
```

What does it do to the logic of code to be so judicious about memory?

It's interesting, because certainly some of the tricks are something you'd have used twenty years ago, but there's all these new mechanisms, and all these new beautiful objects and all this other stuff around it, so it doesn't make the code super unreadable to code that way. It's just something you have to be aware of when you're reading it or modifying it or writing it.

Here's an example. In [Delicious Library] the books are little cards, modeled after playing cards: the idea was a Magic the Gathering card that says, here's your item and here's its little description and its abilities. So each card has a little text field below, and it turns out one of the biggest impediments to my scrolling was drawing that text. There were a few big things that were killing me: one was database access, and one was my naïve imitation scrolling, which would start to create a new card as soon as you scrolled. In creating it, I would create a little image, and then all the text fields below, and there'd be like 25 text fields.

Now, on the Mac, allocating 20 NSTextFields takes, oh, I want to say a billionth of a second. It is unbelievably fast. [On the iPhone] these text fields were resulting in visible stutters, we're talking a tenth of a second stutter, and I would never have guessed it. The Apple engineers had to tell me, you can't do that when you're scrolling, because there's some weird thing where if you allocate any memory during scrolling it screws everything up and it hates you. Every byte. Because we're not talking that many bytes, a couple UI text fields, maybe 40 bytes are lost, literally. That's 25 times 40 [bytes] that I'm allocating, and it just absolutely murders performance.

Here's what I did instead: I created a pool of UI text fields, or whatever they call them, ahead of time, and just pulled out of the pool when I'm scrolling. So the app pulls one out of the pool and sticks it on the screen, and when the other card goes off screen, it recycles all UI text views.

So in your code, what it looks like is, instead of saying, "Hey I'm going to lay out another line, allocating another text view," it looks like, "I'm going to allocate another line, so, hey pool please give me a new text view or create one in the unusual circumstance I've pulled them all out."

Bottom line: the code's still readable, but then somewhere else you've got all this machinery you had to write. These pools where the device can recycle logic and stuff like that. So I had to upgrade to a generic pool handler, which is a great thing to do, honestly, because it turns out this trick is used a lot everywhere in the iPhone. However, in my case I just created it myself as a class.

What's good about this mode of developing?

It's totally self-documenting. The reusing of those fields is never going to be too problematic, and if it was, like some field didn't want to be reused, you can just fix it in one choke point, and you're done.

There was actually one type of object that because of a bug in the 2.0 framework you couldn't reuse. Like, if you tried to use the UIImageView, you could put it onscreen and give it an image, and it would work great; and if you pull it offscreen and give it another image, and put it back onscreen, it just won't draw as second time.

So because of that bug, it's not design-efficient to do things like that. I couldn't put those in pools, so those slow me down a little bit. But as soon as they fix that bug, I was able to go back to the code and enable pooling to that object.

Did designing the iPhone app change the way you view desktop UI?

Yeah it did, actually. When the iPhone just came out, you'd be looking at table view, and then you'd click on something, and that whole table view would slide to the left, and a whole new table would slide in from the right. That was new on the iPhone; that was a really new idea. And I started thinking about that sort of thing in desktop apps: kind of, like, slide out this old thing, slide in all new thing, and have it be animated. I actually pitched it at Omni, after I was there, for OmniGraffle. I pitched it as a way to deal with it some of the clutter they have with their document browser view. They didn't do it. But plenty of good designers will look at what works on the iPhone and see that some of those things they want to add to a bigger device.

What's interesting about the iPhone is that you could make a really, really gorgeous app that does nothing, and people will buy it. And some people, honestly, think Delicious Library is that app. I understand that to some people it's not their cup of tea, and they're like, "Well this is pretty, and people buy it because it's pretty." I take that as a compliment. It's good that they see that first. But obviously there's a lot more.

Part V

Fitting a Big Idea into a Small Space–Keeping the Feature List Focused, Simple, Refined, and Compelling

If the last section was about excellence in execution, this one is about conceptual excellence—the big idea.

This section features Wooden Labyrinth 3D, a life-like game, and Prowl, a notification utility. It'd be hard to find two apps that begin with such diametrically opposed use-cases. Wooden Labyrinth 3D is a time-sucking game that is hard to beat and even harder to put do wn. Prowl, by contrast, is a set-and-forget Growl utility meant to notify users of their computers' activity without taking up their time.

However, both demonstrate an acute awareness on the part of their developers of the way iPhone users interact with their devices. Wooden Labyrinth 3D is based on a classic game requiring the manual manipulation of two knobs to navigate through a wooden maze. Developer Elias Pietilä creates a 3D virtual maze and uses the iPhone's accelerometer-based inputs to make a game that's possibly even more interactive and addictive than the original.

On the other hand, when you see Zac West's Prowl app, you might be tempted to ask, "What's the big idea?" It's minimalist in spirit but incredibly useful for those who want to stay connected with their computer without being chained to it. It's an example of knowing what people want as much as knowing what they need: West built his push notifications with the capability to set quiet hours, customize profiles, and expand functionality. Know your user, these two projects suggest, and the big ideas will come.

Chapter 9

Wooden Labyrinth 3D

Developer Name: Elias Pietilä
Development Company: Elias Pietilä
Tags: Workflow; Fun; Outdoing Copycats
URL: http://qvik.fi/

Elias Pietilä is not a developer. He's not a businessman, either, or even much of a video gamer. To hear him tell it, he's just a student living in the ghetto. "Okay, maybe not the *ghetto*," he says, "but definitely a low quality area near Helsinki."

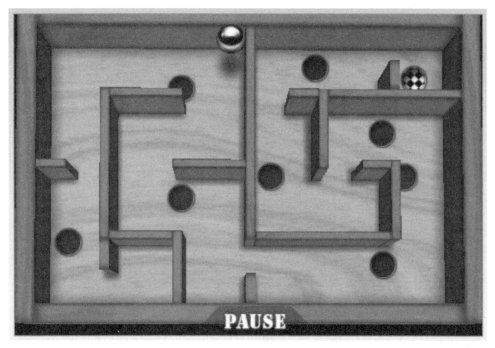

Figure 9–1. *Pietilä's labyrinth shifts perspective as it receives input from the iPhone's accelerometer, creating its three-dimensional effect.*

What Pietilä is, however, is a mathematically talented Mac devotee whose iPhone game, Wooden Labyrinth 3D, has been downloaded almost two million times from the iTunes Store. A slick, addictive incarnation of an ages-old wooden maze game, the paid version of Wooden Labyrinth 3D, seen above in Figure 9–1, had netted him $68,000 USD by the time he earned the 2009 Apple Design Award for best student iPhone application—a period of just four months.

It wasn't supposed to be this way. Before he developed Wooden Labyrinth 3D, Pietilä didn't have an incipient career in programming for the Mac. He wasn't even studying computer science; his concentration at the Helsinki University of Technology is telecommunications science. In fact, when he began writing iPhone games, he wasn't actually in school at all. He was on a year-long hiatus from his Master's program, helping build prototype applications for—of all things—Nokia phones. (Figure 9–2, Nokia's headquarters in Espoo, dubbed Nokia House.)

It's tempting to think of the "student" category of the Apple Design Awards as a minor-league accolade. But the rapid evolution of Pietilä's successes is in many ways more telling of the nature of the iPhone platform than the careers of many of his fellow winners. His ideas for apps were borne of curiosity, not profit; his build was the result of trial-and-error hacking, not daylighting; and his initiative came from nothing more than his 16-year passion for the Macintosh. Accidental successes like WL3D are the only evidence needed to show that the App Store is perhaps the best forum to make a living in today.

Figure 9–2. *Nokia's cultural and economic shadows loom over Finnish smartphone developers.*

The Dropout

When Pietilä initially took his leave of study from University, it was to pursue a full-time job at Finnish software firm Digia, which programmed for Nokia's S60 platform. He had begun work at Digia as a summer intern prototyping in Flash and ActionScript, and when the school year ramped up, they asked him to stay on as full-time employee. He took leave from school and did.

To work in the technology industry in Finland is to be in the shadow of Nokia. The Finnish culture of technological education that has evolved with Nokia—or perhaps, cultivated it—has made Finland one of the most technologically-oriented countries in Europe. Nearly a third of the country's college graduates enter employment in the sciences, many from the country's premier technical university, Helsinki University of Technology. The university, which is abbreviated "TKK," offers 19 degree programs, nearly all of which lead to a six-year Master's level diplomi-insinööri,or "engineer with university dimploma." Elias Pietilä was getting ready for his fourth year of study at TKK towards just such a degree when he accepted the offer from Digia.

Applying for that job, Pietilä had written on his resume that he was could code in Objective-C. "That was a bit of a lie," he admits. "I got some book on it—it was my brother's—and I think I finished the first two tutorials."

In the fall of 2008, after a year working doing Flash for Digia's Nokia projects, Pietilä quit and prepared to take yet another leave of study; he was going to catch up on school work and return to TKK in the spring. The the iPhone SDK came out, and he didn't even bother registering for classes. "Isn't it true that all the computer geniuses drop out?" he laughs.

At the time, the iPhone wasn't even available in Finland—Pietilä was still using his company cell phone, a Nokia E70. When the Apple device went on sale at the end of the summer, Pietilä got one immediately and downloaded the developer kit. "I had never really programmed anything in any C language," he says.

What he did have was experience with Open GL from an introductory C++ class. Open GL ES would later become the lynchpin of Wooden Labyrinth 3D's success, which Pietilä attributes almost entirely to its intuitive 3D look and feel. "Everyone knows the original game labyrinth," he says of the real-life wooden analog. "It's been beaten to death," he adds. Indeed, there was already a labyrinth game in the App Store by July of 2008. But it was the lush 3D play-scape that Pietilä believes drew customers to his game, vaulting it past his competitor's when it appeared in February 2009. Like its real-life wooden counterpart, Wooden Labyrinth 3D consists of an articulated, walled maze and a steel marble. The object: tilt the playing field to guide the marble to toward the end of the maze, avoiding holes interspersed through the maze as traps. In the game, the iPhone's accelerometer takes the place of the wooden knobs that manipulate the box in the real-life version, allowing a user to intuitively roll the ball around the maze by tilting the phone. As the levels get harder, there are more hole traps, requiring more abrupt stops and starts, and more manual dexterity. Increase the level of difficulty, and the ball slides along the playing surface more readily, as if it were greased with graphite. The responsiveness is incredible at all difficulty levels, and the game is instantly addictive—if ultimately maddening at high levels. Wooden Labyrinth 3D wasn't Pietilä's first iPhone app, but he was hardly a veteran when it soared to the #1 spot in the Finnish App Store. His first iPhone app was a game called Pajatzo, seen below in Figure 9–3, an iPhone incarnation of a popular Finnish gambling game found in gas stations and shopping malls—a kind of Scandinavian equivalent of pinball played with gold coins. It sold brilliantly in Finland—though nowhere else—topping the app list in the Finnish iTunes Store and getting Pietilä some media attention. Pietilä was taken aback. "Pajatzo fits very well on the iPhone's screen, and has a 'wow' effect," he says, "but it's not the best game. Yet people's immediate response was: it's cool because it assimilates the real life thing onto a computer," he says. The phenomenon stuck with him.

It was around that time that Pietilä saw a YouTube video, shown in Figure 9–4, demonstrating a brilliant hack for the Nintendo Wii. In it, Johnny Chung Lee of Carnegie Mellon's Human-Computer Interaction Institute discusses how to improvise something he calls a "head-tracking virtual reality display," using a Wiimote and a pair of LED-equipped glasses. Head-tracking, Lee explains, makes 3D games more real by allowing the computer to know the location of your head—and therefore, your viewing angle—relative to the screen. Tracking your viewing angle allows the computer to manipulate a virtual world with the proper motion parallax, making the screen appear uncannily three-dimensional, as though you were looking through a door or window, and not at a flat surface.

Figure 9–3. *Pietilä's first game, Pajatzo, showed him that real-life games could succeed on the iPhone—if they were made realistically.*

The Challenge

Pietilä set out to build a simulator that took advantage of head tracking on the iPhone. "I thought, okay, let's try to calculate the direction you're looking from based on the phone's tilt," he says. By programming for the accelerometer, he found he was able to give the phone enough data about viewing angle to allow it to construct a convincing 3D model. "I didn't plan on making the labyrinth game, I just planned on making demo of that effect," he says.

It was only once he saw the two-dimensional Labyrinth game by Codify AB in the App Store that he realized the proper home for his creation. "It struck me as odd that they didn't make the three-walled walls," he says.

Figure 9–4. *Johnny Chung Lee's head-tracking virtual reality display, as seen on YouTube, prompted Pietilä to imitate head-tracking on the iPhone.*

Pietilä realized that he could trump the original Labyrinth, pictured in Figure 9–5, if he could give it the Pajatzo treatment: graft the real-life game into a slick, attractive package. "Even by autumn last year, it was obvious that there were some developers making money, but it was kinda quiet," he observed. "I thought [Codify AB's] Labryinth hadn't really gotten the love it deserved—their other games seem to have a lot higher production values." He set to work on a new labyrinth game with view-tracking 3D. "I knew that with a little bit of polish, it could really stand out."

Pietilä went to work with the kind of low-overhead essentials that have come to define the grassroots iPhone dev environment. "I only used my home computer, my Mac Pro," he says, "the first model they came out with." Besides Apple's tools—Xcode, Interface

Builder, Instruments and the like—Pietilä's only other standby was Adobe Photoshop. He used Box2D's premade physics engine, applying textures to the head-tracking model he had made earlier.

His incremental approach to Wooden Labyrinth 3D allowed the flippancy of what he was doing—making a copycat app—to escape him. At least at first. "I became a bit worried, because it was a copy," he says. "But I just sort of went ahead and did it."

The whole app, he estimates, took him between 100 and 120 hours of coding and testing, parceled into early morning bursts of discipline. "Most of the developing time on both games was after midnight," he says. "I would be at home, doing other stuff, thinking, 'oh, I should code today, I should develop.' After midnight I'd think: now I have to do it." He'd code from 12am to 5am, he says, and sleep till noon, noting that he believes Finland to be the highest consumer of coffee per capita in the world. (He is right: each Fin consumes an average of 11.4 dry kilograms of the stimulant annually.)

"Now we get to the fun part, where I tell you that I can't actually code or program; I'm more of a hacker," Pietilä says. In a weird testament to the robustness of the iPhone platform, he says he's certain that both his games are leaking memory constantly. "I used to test for leaks when I was making Pajatzo, but then my version of Instruments stopped working," he says, prompting him to quit. Still he says, neither of his apps so far have suffered problems with crashing because of his loose programming style.

"I'm a normal person—I hate memory management," he explains. "You have to be a freak to enjoy that." His humility belies his obvious competency, but he insists that Apple's platform operates as a kind of mistake-eraser. "Compared to other smartphone platforms, iPhone is more of a desktop," he says, "so you get more leeway with things like memory. Usually you have to be careful about that, and it takes being a mathematical wizard. On the iPhone, you can be a normal person and still code." Comparing it to his first area of mastery, he says, "It's a lot like Flash—we've seen a huge explosion in Flash because you have a lot of ready-made action points. You just draw a shape and tell it to move from here to here." Coding for the iPhone isn't quite that easy, he admits, "but you don't have to be a demi-god to understand it."

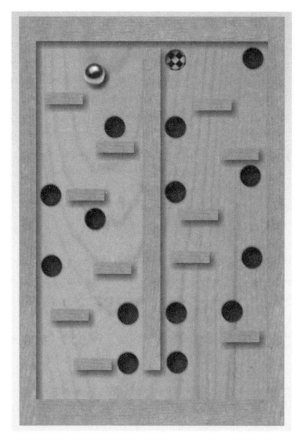

Figure 9–5. *Codify AB's Labyrinth game, which Pietilä set out to beat with his 3-D view.*

Building the Labyrinth

Building Wooden Labyrinth 3D, Pietilä found himself investing just as much time mucking around inside his app as he did writing. "I know a lot of people who can code and compile in 2 hours. I code for two minutes, and I run it and feel around," he says. Due mostly to his impatience, testing was at least 60 hours of his development time, or about half of the total development time, he admits. "I couldn't code for a day and then see what happens," he says. His workflow went in cycles: code, load, space out, and test. "It takes like 30 seconds to build and install the app on iPhone," he explains. "What happens in that 30 seconds: I open my Web browser and then 30 seconds becomes 30 minutes." Reflecting on his workflow, he says sheepishly: "When you're not working for someone, it's hard to keep up your discipline."

Making the process more halting was the fact that his relationship with the game, he says, was a love-hate affair. "The pain of development truly started when I started to make use of the accelerometer data," he says, describing hours devoted to getting the settings dialed for each level of difficulty. "If you want to make the game experience good, you have to run it over and over again to get the feel right, resetting the parameters." The rest of the actual coding process, he says, is relatively benign, if not outright simple. "People think that because you're programming for multitouch that it must be hard. But those effects—they're only a couple of lines of code. You just look it up, and in five minutes you're making yourfirst app."

The "Magic" Piece

All of Wooden Labyrinth 3D is only 5-10,000 lines of code, Pietilä says, and the secret sauce is the 3D perspective effect that he originally designed as a prototype. "[This] piece of code is called every frame to allow the view to distort based on the accelerometer," Pietilä says. What you see below is the code that Pietilä wrote to gather data from the accelerometer and convert it into coordinates for Wooden Labyrinth 3D's virtual camera.

```
-(void) megaPerspective:(double) fovy aspectRat:(double) aspect nearZ:(double) zNear
farZ:(double) zFar lateralDist:(double)lateralDistance
bilateralDist:(double)bilateralDistance
{
                float b;
                float fov;
                float STEREO_FOCAL_LENGTH = 300.0f;
                float STEREO_CAMERA_SEPARATION =lateralDistance;

                /* DO FORMULA CALCULATIONS */
                glMatrixMode(GL_PROJECTION);
                glLoadIdentity();
                fov = fovy / 180.0f * M_PI; // convert FOV to radians

                up = zNear * tan(fov * .5f);
                b = zFar / STEREO_FOCAL_LENGTH;

                left = - aspect * up + (STEREO_CAMERA_SEPARATION * .5f) * b;
                right =  aspect * up + (STEREO_CAMERA_SEPARATION * .5f) * b;
                down = - up;
                up += (bilateralDistance* .5f) * b;
                down += (bilateralDistance* .5f) * b;

                /* SET THE PROJECTION MATRIX FRUSTUM */
                glFrustumf(up, down, right, left, zNear, zFar);

}
```

WL3D's three-dimensional camera makes the game fun to look at, but ultimately any game's playability is determined by the levels of play. Wooden Labyrinth 3D presents players with a nearly limitless array, thanks to an auto-generating level editor. Here, Pietilä explains the algorithm behind his app's other magic piece, the generation engine:

"We start of by dividing the area into a grid of squares—6 x 4 [pixels]—and put walls between these boxes. We then begin at a random square and start "digging" a route in a random direction, removing the wall between those two squares. Then we replace the removed wall with either nothing, a half-wall or a hole. We proceed in random directions until we have visited every square on the board. It's of course rather apparent that we sometimes hit dead-ends. If this happens, we just begin the lottery anew," he says. It takes around 20 to 100 tries for the algorithm to complete a labyrinth where every square is visited. If a random direction yields a visited square or a wall, it attempts to decrement in the other direction before giving up.

"The difficulty is actually the probability of replacing the removed wall with a hole," he says. Since more holes means a harder game, that probability determines the difficulty of the level.

"It's all pretty simple, but the end result is deceptively good-looking and fun to play," he says.

Into the Fray

As of this writing, nearly half the iPhone OS audience lives outside the United States. As an international developer, Pietilä made two smart moves: he sought help in the U.S., which would ultimately help his game's popularity there, but made sure to keep the game appealing primarily to his domestic audience.

When it came time to beta test, Pietilä enlisted the help of an unlikely ally: a 17-year-old kid named Stephen Huber. Pietilä had befriended Huber after the American had posted the first English review of Pajatzo in the iTunes Store, something that Pietilä never thought he'd see because of Pajatzo's dearth of sales in the U.S. Precocious and eager to help, Huber was repaid when Pietilä asked him to help beta test Wooden Labyrinth before its release. Huber went above and beyond the call, uploading video reviews (in English) to YouTube that sparked tons of attention for Wooden Labyrinth when it finally hit the App Store.

When the paid version of the app debuted on February 5, it was priced at $2.99, where it would stay for two months until the Pietilä added the level editor to the package; that boosted the price to $3.99. "Right after I launched my version, they dropped their price from seven dollars to three dollars," he says of Codify AB's app, Labyrinth. Static between the two competing camps developed immediately. "Someone on the forums at TouchArcade[.com] asked them if they dropped their price because they were scared of Wooden Labyrinth 3D," he says. Writing on TouchArcade, developers from Codify AB accused him of copying their game, and not competing on his own merits. "We had words," Pietilä says tersely.

Once Wooden Labyrinth 3D started selling big, Pietilä added AppViz to his suite of tools, to manage his sales statistics. "Apple only provides you with these stupid text files, and you have to import them to Excel, assuming you own Excel, which I don't," he says. AppViz, which is made by developer Ideastorm, works by downloading sales data from every country's constituent App Store for you, then automatically drawing the graphs and pie charts.

The story that AppViz's graphs told Pietilä was a good one. By the time he won his ADA award, the lite version of his star game was still pulling 12,000 downloads a month. The paid version had sold over 35,000 copies at $2.99 or $3.99 a pop.

Even before he won an ADA, Pietilä was enamored of the iPhone SDK. "I'm a true believer, and I don't see anything wrong with it. I think it's pretty goddamn awesome," he says, speaking with particular affection for Xcode. "The package is so well done: you edit the code and press command-enter, and it starts the app directly on the iPhone, checking the values of every field during runtime. It's obviously like that on a desktop, but being able to do that on a mobile is pretty unique," he says, "especially compared to anything that was available on the S60 platform. "After my experience developing for S60, I would never want to do that. Expensive tools, bad channels for selling apps; it just doesn't suit the independent developer."

Pietilä has used his newfound reputation as an iPhone game-maker to work on a new venture he's calling Qvik (pronounced "quick.") The company, which he founded with two classmates, Lari Tuominen and Tuukka Puumala, back when he was an iPhone noob, will provide iPhone consulting and contracting, building custom iPhone apps for businesses.

Pietilä is hoping Qvik will piggyback on Wooden Labyrinth 3D's positive press, but says that he's been careful not to subsume his game under the company brand. Unlike in the U.S., where a unified company facade implies professionalism, Pietilä hypothesizes that Fins prefer to see his surname stay on the games he builds. "There are lots of other Finnish developers that use company names," he says. "But when I made Wooden Labyrinth, I was pretty sure that if I had my name on it, it would attract more media attention." Finland's population is about a quarter the size of the New York metropolitan area at 5.3 million, and its land area is roughly the same size as New Mexico—familiar quarters with a pretty homogeneous population. "It doesn't help if you have crazy-ass software in Finland," Pietilä says. "But if you have a good name, people think it's cute." Having his name on his app, he argues, is part of what helped his games gain national media attention over faceless dev shops like Codify AB.

Pietilä says that European customers will also respond differently to the concept of buying things within an app than have Americans. "In-app purchasing is the lamest thing," he says. "It gives the customer a fake price for the app." Pietilä says that because customers can't adequately judge exactly which features the initial cost of an app actually buys them, they could become disenfranchised. The hidden price of in-app buying will also make comparison shopping for apps harder, he says, which could conceivably drive down prices as unscrupulous publishers figure out ways to hide the true cost of their apps. While some of his American counterparts seem to look forward to in-app buying as a way to monetize new features—features they might have otherwise given away for free with updates—Pietilä maintains that Europeans might find it disingenuous. "Such practices are frowned upon by European trade laws," Pietilä admonishes. Maybe so, but not all developers can afford to forgo monetization options. That's one of the most fascinating things about Pietilä's game; because of its popularity, he can afford to choose a high road and he can stick to it. That's not an assumption that most student developers have the privilege to work under, and it shows that the market for iPhone apps is much more vulnerable to disruptors than is the market for traditional software. Freedom isn't necessarily won by the most elegant UI or the most parsimonious code; it's sometimes simply visceral appeal that can earn developers a following.

Chapter 10

Q&A: Prowl

By Zachary West

Developer Name: Zachary West
Development Company: Zachary West
Tags: Open Source; Push; Release Strategy; Client App
URL: `http://prowl.weks.net/`

Prowl is that rare beast: a truly useful utility for iPhone. It enables iPhone users to send Growl notifications from their Mac or PC to their phone using push notifications, and allows those notifications to be actionable using designated apps. Figure 10-1 shows delivery of one such notification. Want to be notified of a Twitter @reply? Prowl will push it to your phone and open Tweetie for you. If that's not enough, you can use the fully-documented API to build your own implementation; many developers already have, yielding homegrown services for Google Voice, Twitter, and the OS X Dashboard.

Figure 10-1. *Prowl in action, notifying a user of an Adium message.*

But under the hood Prowl is no normal project. Built by Zachary West from a Growl plug-in hack, it required chopping up existing open source, building a server to talk to Apple's Push server, and setting up a Web presence where developers could learn how to program for Growl. Then, of course, there's the local iPhone app itself, a simple array of core options: quiet hours, sounds, and priority settings. In truest iPhone form, Prowl is everything you need, and nothing you don't. West is a lead developer on the open-source Adium project, out of which Growl notifications originated.

How did you get involved with the open source community?

I started doing Objective C programming with Adium, the instant message client. I'm one of the lead developers of the project as of a few months ago. So I started out a few years really working on patches, starting along those lines. The iPhone is basically a mini-Mac, so I could use the same pieces of knowledge that I had from the Mac working on Adium. The hardest part was really coming up with an idea.

I didn't even have a developer account for the iPhone until I'd actually thought of creating Prowl. I was sitting around over the weekend, and realized just what a good idea it was. So I went ahead and paid for the account, and started setting my phone up. A few weeks after I had the idea, it was already up on the app store.

What aspect of the project took the most time?

Prowl took about 400 to 500 hours for the initial version. A lot of the work was on the backend for the web site, because a significant amount of the program is not actually in the iPhone. A lot of it runs independent of the iPhone, either on the person's computer sending to the server, or the server processing the events that are sent from the individual's computer, or the program that is sending the notification. But that's a blessing, because if a random bug pops up, I can usually fix it server-side to either mitigate it on the client on the iPhone, or just avoid it entirely, which is definitely very helpful and a lot different than having to deal with the extremely difficult approval process [by resubmitting the app].

How did you first envision people using Prowl?

My original intention was probably two-fold: firstly, I wanted really to be notified of messages on Adium when I wasn't there. I also wanted to know when torrents finished downloading, because I'm usually out and about, and if something finishes that's taken like 3 or 4 days, I'm usually interested in immediately knowing. So with that in mind, I tried to focus on a way to really have my computer tell me about things when I wasn't there, and Growl was obviously a choice. Growl actually started as an Adium project before I was involved in Adium, so it's kind of a logical progression.

Why use Growl?

I wanted it so that nobody had to do any extra work to use the application—no updates, nothing along those lines. I had to create a Growl plug-in, which integrated kind of seamlessly. But there was really no standard way of doing what I was after; there is an MMS plug-in, but it wasn't quite the same paradigm. So I really wanted to just have it be a part that slapped into Growl without any extra work involved for the user, mostly because I think that would be easier for everybody, but also because it lets anything that uses Growl also use Prowl, without any modifications or redistributions. And what's great is that the Windows Growl clone Snarl and Growl for Windows also adopted the ability to use Prowl. It pretty much just expanded to every operating system without really any programs having to be written for it.

How does the plug-in work?

It declares itself as a style, which in Growl the notifications are received from the application, and then Growl itself will redisplay the notification on the screen to the user. When Prowl receives the notification for display, it checks its preferences and then tells another plug-in to do the actual display, while it goes ahead and sends to the Growl server, so it kind of works itself as a middle man between another Growl style and itself. But one important limitation is that Growl can only display one particular display style, or plug-in, for a particular message—so in order to avoid Prowl being the most annoying program ever and sending every notification only to the iPhone, you have to do a little hacking around, kind of exploiting how Growl works, to allow the messages to be displayed multiple times [on the computer and iPhone].

How do you hack it?

Growl plug-ins are very simple. Basically you just have a few parts: one that talks to Growl, one that sets up the preference window, and another one that does the actual displaying. I looked at some of the other plug-ins, and kind of just went from there. It was mostly just implementing a few functions; obviously, the core of it is a little bit more difficult, dealing with Prowl and all that, but I'd say overall Growl plug-ins are easy to hack.

What Prowl offers is the ability to kind of customize what goes on when it receives the message from a particular application. So originally my goal was to use a system of Growl that, at the time, nobody really used: the priorities for notifications. Really, priorities were just used to change the colors of particular styles and, for the most part, Christopher Forsyth, the project manager for Growl, was kind of pushing for removing them. Nobody really thought of them as a useful feature. But I saw them as really a way to finally bring in the right level of controls to the notifications. I had that control in the option to only send, say, high priority messages from the computer to the Prowl application.

And along those lines, I've added in things like only sending it when the computer is idle. I have few other ideas in my head, like Bluetooth proximity, but I haven't really implemented those yet. Mostly the goal is to try and be more intelligent about sending the notifications when the user doesn't really want them to be sent.

What's unique about the way Prowl uses Push notifications?

When I was writing Prowl, there really weren't a lot of resources to look into the Push notifications. The Apple documentation is good, but it definitely lacks some of the information, like the particular scraping you need to do for the text being sent, things like that. Prowl has to deal with a very wide variety of message-types, so it has to chop the unicode text properly when sending to the Apple server, for example. And the Apple server is very strict about the kind of things it accepts, so if you're wrong at all about the syntax, it will either disconnect you or the client will fail to receive the message. The most complex part of dealing with the Push notifications was just having to deal with an arbitrary text of arbitrary length from users, being sent to something that required a very strict requirement of the type of text displayed. So it's using Push notifications in a broader sense that I think Apple might've envisioned.

What's the 'chain of command' that a notification traverses to get to an iPhone?

Prowl [on the Mac] relays the message to the Prowl server, which then tells Apple to get the Push notification out. Then the user opens the Push notification, or opens the Prowl app, which downloads the notifications from the Prowl server.

It would be nice to avoid the death of having to deal with the Apple's servers, or my server, but it's really just the way it's laid out. It's almost impossible to go any other way.

Apple doesn't let you relay a message from an application directly to its servers?

Right, Apple says that you shouldn't have lots of things connecting [to the Push server] unless you actually need it, and you shouldn't have lots of transient connections either. You can't just open a connection, send a Push notification, and close the connection. I think that'd really be a requirement for an individual computer to connect [without going through the Prowl server]. I'd also have to distribute my SSL certificates, along with the plug-in, in order to connect to the Apple servers.

What's particularly interesting about the way Prowl works?

It does things very simply. Really the only complex thing it does is exploit the ability to relaunch into another application, for which it declares URL types in a particular application. Lots of applications are adding it these days almost specifically for Prowl support too, so that when a notification comes in, the user can be immediately redirected to the appropriate [iPhone] application without having that particular application support Push itself.[1] So nothing really extraordinarily difficult had to be

---

[1] For more about data URLs and a sample project, see Chapter 3 on Topple.

written for the iPhone application itself: it's just a matter of putting the work together, and organizing it in a way that works.

What's tricky about interacting with the Push server?

Originally, it was a little difficult to understand what Apple was expecting in a connection to the Push server. The documentation is there, and the examples are there, but I run into certain problems like the unicode not being cut properly, because I was cutting in the middle of a multi-byte sequence. That's obviously my problem, but it was something that wasn't exactly easy to detect. I'd say a major difficulty was the little unexpected things, like how it expected apostrophes to be escaped, or how some of the text should go through. The server only allows 256 bytes of the data to go to a particular device included inside of a JSON message, which isn't necessarily limiting, but it does make it a little tough to pass the messages around as you'd expect.

How many messages have gone through Prowl to date?

About 7 million, last I counted, were sent through the Prowl server since its release. I think about 13,000 users have downloaded the app, last I checked.

When building a utility, do you think about usability differently than you would for another kind of app?

Originally I just wanted to get the Push notifications working; the UI wasn't necessarily an afterthought, but it definitely was not a priority. I'd have friends of mine yelling at me: "You have to make a good looking application, or else what's the point." And it's true, when it comes to Mac programming and iPhone programming, it's not quite the same discipline as other types of programming; you have to make an application that actually looks good, or else nobody will use it.[2] It's not good enough to be useful—it has to be, "it's useful, it looks good, it works good." So I tried to make Prowl as absolutely as simple as possible, and to keep in mind that its goal was to display a notification. Now of course, displaying notifications, playing what you want, launching other applications, those are all possible—but really the core of it is just displaying notifications. I wanted that concept to be easy to follow, so that was the big consideration when putting everything else together. [Figure 10-2 shows Prowl's preferences, which keep it from harassing the user unnecessarily.]

_____

[2] For more on aesthetics, see Chapter 8 on Delicious Library.

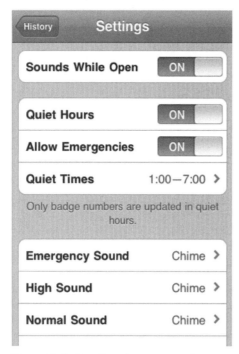

Figure 10-2. *Prowl's preferences pane is sparse but carefully considered.*

How can the open source community add to Prowl's functionality?

I'm adding some features myself: the second-release 1.1, has quiet hours, new sounds—things along those lines. I don't imagine it's going to really expand beyond what it does, but it's definitely going to have new things added to it. What I like about it is using the public API, it allows anybody to expand Prowl really in any way they want. So you have services popping up like pre-fetcher, which does Twitter notifications specifically through Prowl without your computer being on. There are also two or three services for Google Voice, and other things along those lines. I like to keep my mind focused specifically on the notifications themselves. I let other people work on the angles of specific niche items that can be sent through Prowl; I know that if I had to maintain them along with the server and everything, it would just be an overwhelming amount of work. (Figure 11-3 shows some of Prowl's API calls.)

What do you know now about working with Growl that you wish you knew at beginning?

Working with Growl, I probably would have liked better plugging documentation. I separated the project really into three pieces in the beginning. I created nice repositories before any code was written: the Prowl plug-in, the iPhone application, and the web site. Those are all the three major components. They almost have equal share in my mind of what really needs to be done. IPhone applications are very well documented; it just took a long time to do it, of course. The Growl plug-in took a good amount of reading the

Growl code and trying to figure out exactly what it was doing when a notification was received, so that I could kind of duplicate the functionality for how Prowl redisplays into a different style. So, I'd say the major roadblock, toolset-wise, was just trying to understand a program that I myself hadn't written, and really had no experience writing, dealing with the Growl program itself.

Prowl doesn't make use of most of the iPhone's inputs. Is it tempting to add more features?

Yes, but when you add stuff, some users might be drawn to a particular small thing you implement—but if you try to cover multiple bases in a particular application, you generally don't see a user increase proportionate to the amount of things you add. I've had discussions with some other developers about how they looked at things, and really when you're organizing an iPhone application, if you focus on a specific chunk that you want to work on, and you don't try to do extra, you don't think, "Oh this could go in there also, and all that stuff." You just focus on a specific usage set. I also think it's a lot easier for you to tell users about it that way, than if you had 11 different features you had to advertise at the same time.

What about genuinely useful stuff, like the Bluetooth proximity feature you mentioned?

I'm a little bit torn on implementing that. I don't really know the Bluetooth code on Mac very well, but I also don't really want Bluetooth on my phone turned on because it's a battery hog. But I also would like the ability not to be told about Prowl notifications when I'm next to my computer without having to really think about it that much myself. Either Bluetooth proximity, or detecting the phone itself is plugged into a USB port, something along those lines—to really to automate it would be nice. In a perfect world the phone would know that if it was next to the computer. The Bluetooth feature isn't necessarily overreaching—it's kind of a logical extension—but it's a little bit beyond the amount of work I wanted to do for the initial release.

add (POST)

Add a notification for a particular user.

You must provide either **event** or **description** or both.

apikey [204]	Up to 5 API keys separated by commas. Each API key is a 40–byte hexadecimal string. When using multiple API keys, you will only get a failure response if **all** API keys are not valid.
providerkey [40] *Optional*	Your provider API key. Only necessary if you have been whitelisted.
priority *Optional*	Default value of 0 if not provided. An integer value ranging [−2, 2] representing: −2. Very Low −1. Moderate 0. Normal 1. High 2. Emergency Emergency priority messages may bypass quiet hours according to the user's settings.
application [256]	The name of your application or the application generating the event.
event [1024]	The name of the event or subject of the notification.
description [10000]	A description of the event, generally terse.

Figure 10-3. *Prowl's API has opened up the app to some surprising third-party inventions.*

How important is Prowl's Web interface?

There's basically two parts of the web site: what people see, and what the application deals with. As I was writing the iPhone application and the Growl plug-in and the web site, almost parallel, really they had to support what everybody else was expecting. So the Growl plug-in expected to be able to send notifications, the iPhone application expected to be able to receive them, and the web site was kind of the joining force between those two ends. Of course I also had to create a web site that was marginally attractive, and I'm obviously not good web developer, but I try. It had to be attractive and usable, so I tried to keep the organization as specific as possible to what users would be doing: logging in, and either changing settings or adding notifications. So advertising these features on the front page is obviously important.

When I first wrote the application I didn't even think of a public API. People started requesting it, and I thought it was a really good idea, and now that's one of the driving forces of the web page also. So even though users are really using the App Store to find applications, I'd say having a reputable, usable web page definitely helps the process.

How has the API changed the way you think about Prowl's usability?

The goal was a very simple API that has two or three features, adding notifications, and checking whether or not one of those API keys was valid, which has allowed Growl for Windows and Snarl to add public API-use functionality, along with all the various web services and tie-ends that people are using with Prowl.

I'd say a few days of work definitely went into the API. Really I just wanted it to work in a way that would allow anybody to send notifications to the Growl servers without any extra steps. It's just a basic HGDP post-API that allows you to specify what's displayed in Prowl. But you can also just specify what user receives the message using an API key functionality, so a user doesn't necessarily have to give a third party their username and password.

Originally Prowl was meant just specifically for Growl notifications, but it kind of evolved more into a universal Push notification system after release. It definitely evolved into one of the leading features that allows pretty much anything to happen beyond my imagination, without me having specifically to do it myself.

Has Prowl created a new usage scenario for the iPhone, or replaced an extant scenario that was too clunky?

Well, there are two or three specific web services that revolve around Prowl, and there are also things like a WordPress plug-in that are kind of new. Some people are also just using the command line script to the notifications from particular web site monitoring, or running a rule set that forwards to Prowl on certain events. It's difficult for me to keep up, because unless they really tell me about it I don't really know what's going on. So from my perspective, people are using it for pretty much everything they were using SMS notifications before—but instead of having to pay SMS fees it just goes through Prowl. Nice, simple, fast.

What are some of the most interesting usage scenarios you've come across?

Some of the really awesome ones revolve around weather monitoring. My favorite ones are definitely in Japan: they are using earthquake monitoring going through Prowl, so you get notified of any earthquakes or something along those lines. Other people there are using it for subways delays, things like that. Some of the usages in Japan I didn't even think were possible, but they just aggregate so many sources though Prowl.

How did you arrive at that $2.99 price-point?

I envisioned in my mind somewhere between $3.00 and $4.00, because I have to support it forever, and I have to deal with the bandwidth costs and the server costs. A lot of the 99 cent applications don't necessarily have huge margins cause you're only getting 70 cents out of it. I also knew for sure I didn't want to support a 99 cent application, because I think the mindset of somebody buying a 99 cent application is:

"Oh I can use it and complain as much as I want, and I'm still owed everything from everybody." I think that segment of the particular marketplace is a little bit more work.

So the price point keeps the app in the hands of the l33t, so to speak?

Yeah, definitely the 99-cent buyers are a lot more difficult to please than someone who is buying a more expensive application. I really wished to avoid the users that would not really understand what they are buying because it requires Growl. If you don't read that text, you're not likely to understand why nothing's happening on your phone. So when something is a little more expensive they are more intent to understand what they're buying before they actually go and do the purchasing.

Is Prowl profitable?

It's definitely making money. It's worked out very nicely; I'm very happy with the response of people purchasing Prowl. The server costs are lower than my income, and the servers are running spectacularly under this specific load. I think I could scale it two or three times more, but I haven't even to think about adding more servers, which is always very easy to do with the way I have it set up in the backend.

Is there a lesson to other developers in Prowl?

It's incredibly important thing to just understand what you're actually trying to do. Not overreaching is really important when you're developing a small application that isn't necessarily meant to be used all the time. With a utility, you really have to understand exactly what it can (and should) be used for. You don't want to add annoyances, or unnecessary steps; focus on your main usage above than anything lse.

Part VI

Making Better Apps and Enfranchising Your Users –The Right Way to Iterate, Planning an App Store Strategy, and Some Serious iPhone Development Philosophy

The following chapters are more free-associative than the preceding ones, but no less practical. All three of the developers in this section have created successful iPhone apps: Smule's have topped the App Store on several occasions; Instapaper is a favorite of web addicts everywhere and its API features in popular apps like Tweetie and iReddit; and Toronto developer MarketCircle won a 2009 Apple Design Award (ADA) for its Mac app Billings 3, and is now working on an iPhone version of that app.

But in addition to winning approval from users and from Apple itself, these developers have also spent more time than most considering--and speaking out about--the peculiarities of the device and its ecosystem. Reading these chapters will allow you to spend more time coding and less time struggling with approval, updates, customer service, motivation, pricing, and sales. They'll also give you three design philosophies you can adapt, study or react against.

Marco Arment, lead developer of Tumblr and creator of Instapaper, is particularly deft at cutting through some of the so-called "common knowledge" sophistry that clouds the platform. Wang, who co-founded Smule, makers of hugely popular musical apps, shares his holistic ideas keeping inspiration and creativity central to the development process. And Brandon Walkin and Alykhan Jetha of MarketCircle discuss how they've successfully iterated through three versions of Billings and brought the final version mobile.

While we're feeling philosophical: why are the developers in this book developing for this platform, anyway? What can we learn from the iPhone itself? This chapter dives into those questions headlong, and ferrets out how small teams and slow deliberate timelines have fomented not only these developers' success, but Apple's.

Chapter 11

User Experience: Ge Wang

Developer Name: Ge Wang
Development Company: Smule
Tags: Connectivity; Workflow; Fun
URL: http://smule.com

Ge Wang is a professor of music and computer science at Stanford University, where he oversees the Stanford Laptop Orchestra at the university's Center for Computer Research in Music and Acoustics (CCRMA, pronounced karma). Wang is also the cofounder of Sonic Mule, lovingly known by its team as Smule, which has built several phenomenally successful musical iPhone apps from Ocarina, a virtual flute, to I Am T-Pain, a vocalizer that imitates the popular Auto-Tune software used in hip-hop post-production.

Like Ngmoco, featured in Chapter 3, Smule has managed to turn the iPhone into a creative conduit where users can play, learn, and perform. Also like Bob Stevenson's team, Wang's engineers and artists have managed to reinvent Smule's trademark aesthetic and play in a litany of new ways, creating a family of bestselling apps. As with Topple 2, players can fire up Smule apps such as Ocarina or Leaf Trombone (shown in Figure 11–1) and recognize the seed of the challenge, but still revel in its new and creative implementation.

Smule's apps are also an education in connectivity. Each instrument they create is more deeply enmeshed with other players, in ways that beget creative sharing and competition alike. At heart, friendly rivalry is the lure that keeps both Smule's and Ngmoco's players coming back, long after they've become inured to the gorgeous art or the novelty.

Unlike other developers, though, Wang and his team have recognized and considered the iPhone first and foremost as an object, not simply a computing platform for software. In Wang's hands, the iPhone has become a compact instrument; the phone's guts, the code, even the visual design melt away.

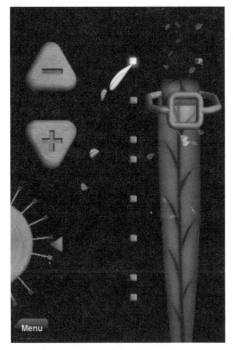

Figure 11-1. *Leaf Trombone's user interface. The player blows into the phone's mic to create a sound, which can be modulated by sliding the leaf-scrubber on the right-hand side of the screen.*

What is your background like?

I'm a computer music researcher. What I liked about both disciplines was that I could be truly creative. The act of programming, I believe, can be and should be an extremely creative endeavor; not only do you get the wonder and the joy of building things, but you get to craft, build, and then express. That's also why I love music. But with music, there's an emotional aspect that touches people in a universal way.

Our apps are panoplies of both [music and programming]. Everything from graphics, numerical analysis, programming, design, networking—all of these things go into every one of our apps. On the musical side, we are exploring the rules of Western tonality, how we can bend and break them, emotionally and psychologically, and how we can convey that to other people. Both fields are extremely rich. At some point in grad school it occurred to me that I could combine the two. And that's how I started at computer music research [as a student] at Princeton.

Why did you bring your research from computers to the iPhone?

I started as a professor at Stanford in September of 2007, first in music and eventually in computer science. When I first came to Stanford I had absolutely no plans to found a company.

Right after I started, I met Jeff Smith. He had been the CEO of several startup companies and was going back to Stanford for music composition; he's an excellent pianist and a great composer.

That spring I was actually working on an extension of my dissertation at Princeton, a music programming language called ChucK. I knew that the fact that the iPhone is always connected would make it a truly revolutionary computing platform. It's the most personal computing platform we have today: it's the first piece of technology I use in the morning, and it's the last one I use before going to sleep at night. It's my alarm clock, my time waster, my motivator: in fact, the alarm clock isn't actually what wakes me up. It's only when I check my email—and panic—that I finally get out of bed. That level of intimacy made it clear that [the iPhone] aligned with my mission as a researcher. I had to do it.

Why is the iPhone unique that way?

It's not, entirely. We tried an experimental mobile phone orchestra [using Nokia N95s] around the same time that the iPhone came out. I was really pondering the super-smartphone, the modern smartphone. I was realizing that we might be at an inflection point of computing. We have these powerful compact devices that are intimate and personal.

But with the iPhone, we have multi-touch, an onboard speaker, CPU, GPU, mic, networking, and GPS. There is also this minimalism; the form factor is already there. A real, live ocarina is really no bigger than an iPhone. It's one of the smallest, simplest instruments we know of. (See Figure 11–2, a real ocarina.)

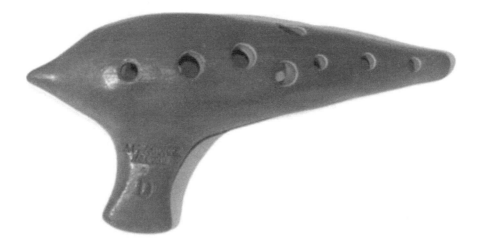

Figure 11–2. *A modern ocarina. The earliest of the instruments are believed to date back 15,000 years. Because they do not rely on their length to produce their tone as flutes do, but instead create their sound from the resonance of the whole cavity, there is no standard length for an ocarina, and the placement of the holes—there are usually between four and twelve—is irrelevant and variable. (Photo credit:* http://de.wikipedia.com*)*

We got to start fresh with iPhone. The design process here [at Smule] is one that doesn't involve cramming or porting. We do not want to take an existing experience and put it on the phone. We try to have the discipline to say, "What is available that we can use?" It's an "inside out" design approach. We didn't try to cram a large instrument into the phone; instead, the process was more looking for a sweet spot where we wouldn't have to sacrifice something. In the process, we realized this is more than a miniature computer. It's a thing unto itself. (Figures 11–3 and 11–4 are early mockups of Ocarina and show how Wang and his engineers mapped musical notes to the button layout.)

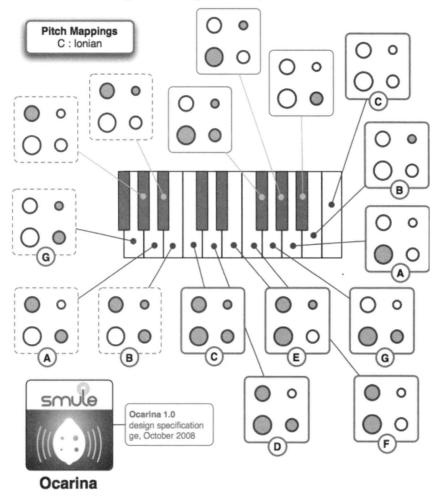

Ocarina

Figure 11–3. *Ocarina uses just four finger "holes" but can produce a range of musical notes.*

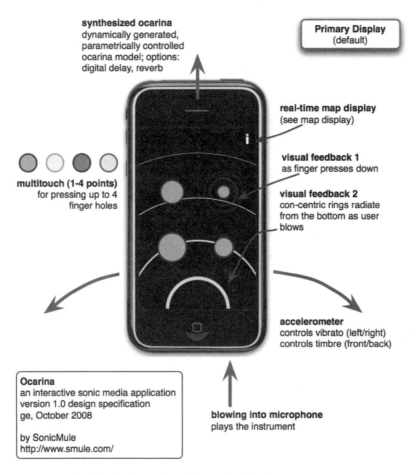

synthesized ocarina
dynamically generated,
parametrically controlled
ocarina model; options:
digital delay, reverb

Primary Display
(default)

real-time map display
(see map display)

visual feedback 1
as finger presses down

multitouch (1-4 points)
for pressing up to 4
finger holes

visual feedback 2
con-centric rings radiate
from the bottom as user
blows

accelerometer
controls vibrato (left/right)
controls timbre (front/back)

Ocarina
an interactive sonic media application
version 1.0 design specification
ge, October 2008

by SonicMule
http://www.smule.com/

blowing into microphone
plays the instrument

Figure 11–4. *Mapping the interaction design behind Ocarina.*

How do Smule apps create music?

We can use ChucK to synthesize sound and to design sounds and interactions. It offers a really graphic turnaround of how a sound might turn out. There's actually a mini ChucK engine running on each phone. The microphone and buttons generate signals that ChucK analyzes with signal processing, extracting information like how hard are you blowing, then deciding to generate sound that is rendered out the speaker. ChucK handles both the interaction and the sound. (Figure 11–5 shows the ChucK operator symbols).

Figure 11–5. *the ChucK operator symbols.*

We built on what we knew from doing laptop orchestras at Stanford and Princeton, where we were essentially building completely new instruments on the laptop. In our instruments, there are equal doses of computer and human; the same is true for both the laptop orchestra and the iPhone.

Building the ChucK engine involved writing a ton of code. I am very much a C and C++ programmer, but transitioning was straightforward. A lot of our audio work on the iPhone has ended up being in C++; in the iPhone SDK you can write all C languages in the same project or even same file, so it was pretty easy to mix to three.

Listing 11–1 is a simple project in ChucK that allows a user to dither some user-generated audio input, perhaps from an iPhone microphone.

Listing 11–1. *A Simple ChucK project*

```
// dither.ck
// demo of dithering
//
// can use any UGen as source in play_with_dither()
// qbits : number of bits to quantize to
// do_dither : whether to dither
//
// gewang

// patch
Impulse imp => dac;

// sine wave generator
SinOsc s => blackhole;
220 => s.freq;

// go
play_with_dither( s, 2::second, 6, false );
play_with_dither( s, 2::second, 6, true );
.5::second => now;

play_with_dither( s, 2::second, 5, false );
play_with_dither( s, 2::second, 5, true );
.5::second => now;
```

```
play_with_dither( s, 2::second, 4, false );
play_with_dither( s, 2::second, 4, true );
.5::second => now;

// dither
fun void play_with_dither( UGen src, dur T, int qbits, int do_dither )
{
    // sanity check
    if( qbits <= 0 || qbits > 24 )
    {
        <<< "quantization bits out of range (1-24)", "" >>>;
        return;
    }

    // loop
    float sample;
    int quantized;
    (1 << 24) => int max;
    while( T > 0::second )
    {
        // get the last sample
        src.last() => sample;
        // quantize it
        if( do_dither ) // dither
            ((sample + Std.rand2f(0,Math.pow(2,-qbits))) * max) $ int => quantized;
        else // no dither
            (sample * max) $ int => quantized;

        // throw away extra resolution
        quantized >> (24-qbits) << (24-qbits) => quantized;
        // cast it back for playback
        (quantized $ float) / max => imp.next;
        // advance time
        1::samp => now;
        // decrement
        1::samp -=> T;
    }
}
```

What did you learn doing laptop orchestras that informed your iPhone app design?

The nice thing about computers is their generality. With laptop orchestra, we can build instruments that are tailored for experts or people who don't have much traditional training. There's a really nice spectrum of instruments. Every time we add a new piece to the orchestra, we redesign the whole thing [to be consonant]. The curse is that we have to start over every time, but we have a fundamental say in how the instrument works and sounds. Basically, we learned what was possible along a massive spectrum.

The instruments in laptop orchestra are meant for people who have experience with laptop orchestra, not necessarily experience with real instruments; we have both novices and expert musicians in that play with us. Some instruments pretty much deconstruct and reconstruct the actions of a traditional instrument by modeling the interactions of all parts of the instrument, and connecting them to parts of sound generating algorithms. Others are more bizarre. Ultimately, all the instruments are out of this world. The way you "play" them also varies. On one you might bow your finger across the track pad while manipulating the wind with thekeys.

Before you began building apps, were there any that you particularly admired?

One app that I really loved was Fieldrunners. It's one of the earliest games. It was clearly built with such quality, tender love, and care. These soldiers come marching [at your gate] and your job is to shoot them down. The graphics are inviting, the interaction is fluid, and it's my number-one most played game on the iPhone. That's saying a lot, since it's the first and last piece of technology I use during my day. Whether I am waiting in line, or just have some downtime, the phone is right there.

Are Ocarina and Leaf Trombone games?

A game or a tool—I'm not sure what [they are]. There is a game element to them. I'd say it's a new type of computer-mediated social musical instrument. But it's built on this belief that everyone is inherently creative, and that by setting the conditions right, we can unlock creativity in anyone. Music is great for this, because it's hard to find someone who hates music. That's the social component. There's also the spontaneity; the sound is synthesized right on the phone, its not prerecorded—that's another social component. People can actually play an instrument for the first time on the iPhone. And people are doing it; we've had 20 million shared performances and over a million downloads. If you told me a year ago that a million people would be blowing into their phones to create music, I would have thought it was a real stretch.

How have your apps built on each other?

Sonic Lighter was the first app. You can light it by flicking your fingers, or by holding it up to another phone—social "lighting." One phone emits a sound and another phone hears it.

If there's one app that influences the rest, it's Sonic Lighter. We had the globe in there, so you could see lighters all over the world. Leaf Trombone (pictured in early mock-up drawings in Figure 11–6) is definitely our most sophisticated app to date; it has really taken social experience to a new level. You can give each other feedback on your playing. We've had more than 400,000 judging sessions now.

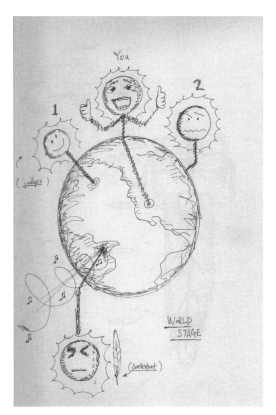

Figure 11–6. *Early drawings of Leaf Trombone showed the competition globe featuring prominently.*

How do you know how difficult to make an instrument?

We try to make them absolutely as accessible to as many people as possible, but without losing the possibility for virtuosity. We don't want to make it just for expert musicians, but we want the expertise to be the goal. If someone practices at an instrument, they can get better at that it; we try to make our apps the same way. We try to cover all the bases here. There's a YouTube video of one user playing Oh Shenandoah, and she really plays it beautifully. We were like, "Wow."

It's not all about playing, though. Sometimes it's about listening. We had a review from a soldier in Iraq; in the few nights he has off, he said he takes out his iPhone and listens to music with Ocarina, and that it's really peaceful in the midst of all this chaos. To see someone from Japan play Amazing Grace, or hear the Star Wars theme from Jamaica—there's something poignant about it. (Figure 11–7 shows the Smule globe as it appears in Ocarina, which allows users to listen to other players all over the world.)

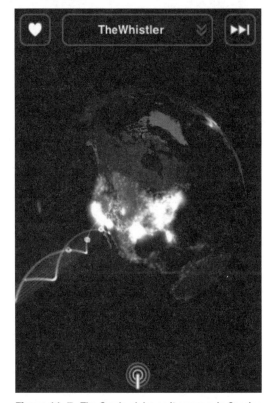

Figure 11–7. *The Smule globe as it appears in Ocarina.*

What do you have in mind when you set out to build a new Smule app?

Well, we named the company Sonic Mule after my favorite sci-fi characters, the Mule from Isaac Asimov's Foundation Series. He's not the nicest of characters; he could use special powers to influence millions of people. In some ways that's what we want from our apps. We want to bring what we can do with computers and music to a wide audience to change the way people play music, listen to music, and interact through the vehicles of expressive audio.

Basically, we're trying to build things that people didn't know they liked to do.

Chapter 12

Iterative Design

Developer Name: Alykhan Jetha and Brandon Walkin
Development Company: Marketcircle
Tags: Iteration; Client App; Team Development; Visual Design
URL: http://marketcircle.com

"It never occurred to me that it would be so tough for us," says Alykhan Jetha, the founder of Marketcircle. "But time was more of a deciding factor in Billings than anything else." Of course, time is a factor in all invoicing applications; you can't charge clients in hectares.

But the extra consideration that has gone into Billings 3, shown in Figure 12–1, and its companion app Billings Touch, make both apps case studies in iterative design.

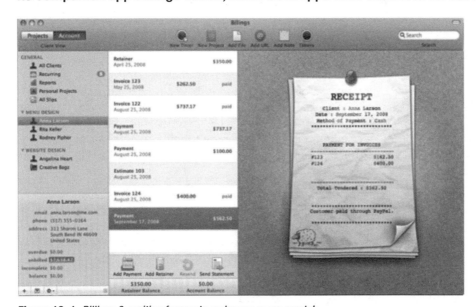

Figure 12–1. *Billings 3, waiting for you to make you some scratch.*

But Jetha, or "AJ" as most people call him, isn't talking about billable hours. And he's not talking about the urgent kind of time right before a looming deadline. He's talking about a much more whimsical version: time to stew.

Unlike most of the apps that Mac users see and use every day, Billings 3 and its companion iPhone app Billings Touch exist under the principle that time takes productivity, not the other way around. It's an app that knows when you're working and when you're not, and it can tell you when to stop working and bill somebody on schedule. And it has to be intuitive, meticulous, streamlined, and steadfast, because it's not just another productivity tool: when it comes to invoicing apps, a bum feature or confusing workflow means literally screwing with users' livelihoods. When Billings is done bouncing in your dock, time isn't *of* the essence. It *is* the essence.

Fitting, then, that it would be the clock—not technical prowess, inspiration, or any number of more nebulous ingredients—that would be Billings' perennial threat. It started, says AJ, with Billings 2. "There was a tremendous amount of debate about workflow back then," he says. "One of our developers at the time was an interaction expert. So we went back and forth with him trying to find a good medium, but ultimately development stopped for a good two or three weeks," he says. Work pushed on, but problems bubbled up. "We'd get into heated debates, taking off more weeks to hash out ideas. Then we'd come back to the original idea, and that's how we'd know it was right."

Billings 3, which launched in September 2008, was burdened by the same democratic stalling, but it may have been the secret to the app's success. "A lot of times customers make requests, but if you dig deeper and ask for the use cases behind them, you find they don't necessarily know what they're asking for," he says, echoing other developers in this book. "What appears to be the solution initially isn't always the best solution. If you jump in, you might miss more elegant ways of solving a problem." And elegance is what wins customers—and ADAs.

The Canadian Way

In a chapter about iterative design, it's only fitting to start at the beginning. The Marketcircle of 2009, winner of its second little silver cube from Apple in June's WWDC, is a capable 25-person Mac development shop based in an office just outside Toronto, in Markham, Ontario. They're consummate software pros today, but it's tempting to make an ancestral link between the company's deliberative process and its hapless stumble into Mac development in 1999.

Americans like to stereotype Canadians as a bunch of friendly, bandying socialists in Uncle Sam's attic, and the founding of Marketcircle happens to feel particularly Canadian. They didn't start selling software for the Mac because they thought they could get rich, or because they were hardcore enthusiasts of the platform. Simply put, they started selling Mac software because Apple deigned to ask them to, and they said yes. Because they're nice guys like that.

Marketcircle was initially founded as a Web startup in 1999, at first with AJ as the lone employee and soon after with Michael Clark as the VP of engineering. But the timing was inauspicious. Their .com startup, a marketplace where buyers and sellers could negotiate instead of bid at auction, never won venture funding, and when the tech bubble burst, they turned to web consulting and then software development ("to catch our breath," says AJ). It was a pretty easy transition; the web work they had planned on doing was object-based, and AJ himself had been developing object-based applications for the NeXTStep platform doing large system data analysis since 1990. In 1997, Apple bought out Steve Jobs' second startup, and NeXTStep began its metamorphosis into Cocoa. So in 2002, when it was clear that Marketcircle needed to build an in-house business management program to manage its consulting clients, they built it for the Mac instead of for NeXTStep (the program, Daylite, is shown in Figure 12– 2). "Up until 1997, I didn't know anything about the Mac," says AJ.

Figure 12–2. *Daylite, Marketcircle's first app, also has an iPhone companion called Daylite Touch.*

Daylite, as their internal management app came to be called, wasn't meant for public consumption. Then Cupertino came calling. "Apple got wind of it and asked us to sell it," says AJ. The Mac-maker was hoping to rebuild its developer base app by app. "They saw the internal app that we used as a showcase, which was meant for customization. We had already built the app. Their argument was, 'Hey it's not that much more work to make it available to market,'" AJ recalls. Apple pre-iPod was a humbler beast, and AJ says they asked nicely. "It wasn't an arm-twisting kind of thing," he says, "it was a logical argument." As contractors, Marketcircle was used to building specialized systems for highly technical users, but on the Mac, they would be dealing with a horizontal market. "We knew the users were more discerning about interface. We weren't prepared for that. It turned out to be a lot of work."

They agonized over building an interface that end users could make sense of, and their efforts paid off. In 2002 they were granted an runner-up ADA for Daylite 1, and by 2004, they were doing enough business selling Daylite to small businesses that they could afford to quit contract work. In 2005, they reasoned it was time for a sophomore product. "We were already in small business space, so that narrowed it down to small business applications," he said of their brainstorming sessions. "We had a tremendous number of requests for time-billing with Daylite, and I felt like we could do a better job that what was out there." The company's crash course in interface design had heightened their sensitivity to the software marketplace, and they saw a gaping opening. "One of our motivations was that all the invoicing [applications] then—all those apps look like crap. We wanted an app that produced good looking invoices." AJ's working definition of interactivity is as follows: "intuitive use of what's important on the screen." To hear him tell the story, the original version of Billings had its head on straight, but possessed almost none of that interactive aptitude. "We had a very specific market and specific target, but we stumbled at the beginning. Billings 1 was ... a first step," he says haltingly, "but it wasn't anything a lot of people would buy. It wasn't until we hit Billings 2 that we got the interaction semi-decent."

Simply Complex

What makes Billings such a knot of problems is, paradoxically, its simplicity. An invoicing application is, conceptually, perhaps one of the simplest applications that any knowledge worker will use on a daily basis—AJ compares it to iCal, calling it "deceptively deep." At its core, it's a stopwatch; wrapped around the stopwatch are features that let you take the time you log and turn it into proof of billable hours. The forefathers of the generic invoicing app are the dumb standbys of the industrial era: the log-book, the punch-clock. So how did things get so complicated?

The problem may lie in the disparity between what the user expects of the app—to get them paid—and the very specific fields of information that the app needs to do its job: addresses, phone numbers, rates, schedules, dates, times, estimates, and receipts. When you sit down to use, say, CAD software, you expect a learning curve. But something so conceptually intuitive as timed billing needs a low barrier of mastery for users—encounter a little bit of cognitive load using a "simple" billing app, and you begin to feel like a moron. Needless to say, that's not what you want in a user experience. "Billings is a very focused app, with a smaller problem-area than Daylite," AJ says, "but between versions one and two, we had many more discussions about the workflow," which AJ says wasn't much of a focus in version 1.0. "[Talks] lasted for weeks until we found something that we all agreed upon." At the time, the team was just AJ, two developers, and two other engineers dividing their time between Daylite and Billings. (Since then, the company's Billings dev team has swelled as high as seven, with three developers minimum on the project at all times.)

In figuring out just why Billings' workflow became such an engineering knot, there's much to be learned from Marketcircle's head user experience designer, Brandon Walkin. Thoughtful and precocious, he has been at Marketcircle since 2007, when he left a computer engineering program at the University of Waterloo after losing interest in his undergraduate degree. Walkin didn't study art, design, or even computer science—though he says he took one class in C#—but is wholly responsible for most of the interface makeover that went into Billings 3. He was left alone at the switch after just four months on the job as Billings' junior interface guru. His boss, the company's original interface designer, absconded to Google. "They hired me for user interface design," he says, "but I had never done any proper UI design. They hired me based on interview." Walkin wasn't a total user experience noob. At the time, he was running a site called IndieHIG, a kind of wiki that built upon Apple's human interface guidelines. "They didn't update that article for a really long time," he says of Apple's HIG site, "so I started a project for the community to contribute new guidelines." (Later, he realized that the real problem was that AppKit, the Cocoa Application Framework, wasn't being updated with new UI elements as they were introduced in Apple's own apps. More on that later.)

Just a couple of years before, Walkin was far from contemplating Apple's user experience; in fact, he was sure that he wanted to do Windows IT work full-time as a career. "IT work was all I ever did," he says, "and I had this really expensive PC at the time." As a resume-builder he bought a Mac in 2005. "I was just interested in it because I wanted to gain experience with the platform," he says. "It was a PPC Mac Mini, and it was the slowest thing ever. But I ended up being so much more productive on this super-slow machine that I ended up selling my pimped-out PC and going full Mac," he says.

For someone so influential to the look and feel of Billings 3, Walkin says he was woefully out of touch with the world of design when he arrived at Marketcircle. "It was a really steep learning curve," he says. "I had taste; I could recognize what looked good and what didn't, from a visual perspective. But I didn't have much knowledge of interactive, user-centric design," he says. His boss, Adam Baker, trained him on the basics of Photoshop and interaction design. When Baker left for Google, Walkin was thrown into his former boss' management role, taking the interface development lead for Billings 3. "When I got hired, I had started learning about Objective C. I got some books, but I couldn't actually make something working," he says. "Once I started working at Marketcircle, six months in, I started really trying to build something."

One of the masterworks that Walkin says was formative in his interface training was Checkout, the point-of-sale application made by Dutch developers Sofa, who also won a 2009 ADA for their desktop app, Versions. "They're extremely talented—the interaction design is well thought out, and the visual design is stunning," Walkin says. "Take the icon work; it's second to none. If you just go through their apps bundle and look at the icons at 512 pixels it's just unbelievable." (Sofa's app Checkout, is pictured in Figure 12–3, and its Disco app icon in Figure 12–4.)

Figure 12–3. *Sofa's interaction and visual design are "stunning," says Walkin.*

Figure 12–4. *Sofa's iconography is the object of much admiration at Marketcircle and elsewhere.*

But how did Checkout get so good? For that matter, how did Apple itself get so good?

The guys at Sofa have their theories about both. Jasper Hauser and Koen Bok, two of the Sofa ten (counting the cat), echo the Marketcircle guys, but with a corollary: good design takes time, but also the discipline to be jealously protective of your final product. Experiment as much as you want with awful, abominable iterations, they say, but never let the customer see your dirty laundry. "I think even Apple works this way," says Hauser. "I think Apple does a lot of iterative designing where the first initial versions have some nasty interaction shit," he says, but they don't let timelines or "goals" force that stuff onto shelves. "You can feel free to make some bad stuff, but you have to make sure that whatever goes out the door is good."

"The majority of the stuff we make here sucks, and the interaction is horrible," Hauser says, "but we work on it long enough at some point that we're all happy with it. But that takes a lot of time and a lot of effort and a lot of iteration to go beyond that point, to get to where you're happy with it and it works," he says. "That's the only way to do it. It's not some magic thing that happens every time you touch Photoshop or start coding a project."

Bok believes that Apple owes its own successful iteration to the way it responded to its near-failure in the 1990s. Instead of reinventing the Mac in one product cycle, the company adopted a decade-plus iterative schedule for Mac OS X. "They had the option of restarting their entire OS, and they had some very visionary people onboard. They kept all the good parts from the old OS, and while it was technically a step forward from the old OS, the UI was just ridiculously different than the old Macs," he says. "But they took it slowly, and it caught on, also because they had great industrial design that matched the UI design stuff," he says. Time not only allowed Apple to avoid missteps with OS X, but to bring its entire product line in sync.

Their carefully-developed products earned them a "kind of avant-garde crew," Bok says, that made Macs—and Mac development—more lucrative. "If you sell a PC, its target audience is maybe twenty times as big as the Mac's, but it's pretty tough to sell some copies of software there," he says. "The people that are on the Mac are, for whatever reason, very willing to give you ten bucks for beautifully a designed app. Maybe it's because they're richer, or maybe because they respect UI design more. But if you can make a living from it, suddenly it becomes interesting to a lot of talented people," he says.

Those talented people caused a groundswell of good design. "That [market] sparked the idea of being an 'independent developer,'" says Bok, "which is basically the closest thing [a developer] can get to a rock band." The haute market for software gave Mac developers the ability to quit their day jobs, Bok says, and suddenly they had enough time and money to concentrate on usability. As other chapters in this book have shown, revenue and design are inextricably linked; earning money gives you the time and freedom to let the designs stew until they are truly ready.

That time, Bok says, necessarily results in a more personal, opinionated product, which adds even more to the software's appeal. "With these kind of apps, you can kind of have a 'look in the kitchen,' if you know what I mean," Bok says. "With those developers it is very enjoyable to buy an app from them because you really feel like you are a part of this culture that respected the best possible design in software." As Elias Pietilä theorized in Chapter 9 of this book, it was partly his last name that caused his app to sell so well; people found it "cute" that he was just one person, not a faceless company. "It's a mix between supporting your local artist and supporting your local grocery store," Bok says. "It's helping you, the customer, to beat the big companies."

The superiority of small development teams is one of the underlying, if unintentional, conceits of this book. "If you look in general at software from small companies, it has that personal feel," Hauser adds. "You almost have the sense that you bought it from the guy himself. If you buy from big companies like Microsoft or even Adobe, there is no personality attached to it." Apple is no exception, he says. "Everyone who talks about

Apple day-to-day has Steve [Jobs] in his mind; there's still some real personality in mind," he says.

Sofa, like Marketcircle, is a small company. Look at other prized dev shops in the Mac community—Boinx, Cultured Code, Potion Factory, Red Sweater, FlyingMeat—and you see similar business models: small groups of tight-knit talents perfecting a handful of careful, beautiful products. The people behind these companies lay much of the praise for their design at Apple's feat: the Cocoa API creates gorgeous apps, they say, or Interface Builder makes aesthetic consistency easy. But little is said about the institutional efficiency and single-mindedness that is available in a small team, and what a profound effect that has on software for the Mac. Apple—who, by most measures, is its own biggest developer, aside from Adobe—is due credit for making development for Mac OS X cheap and easy. But it has also benefitted from the sanctitude of second place, as Bok implies; while Microsoft was struggling to get out of the way of its own success earlier this decade, Apple was quietly—and personally—encouraging talented developers like Marketcircle to build fluid, thoughtful applications for Mac OS X, without any of the cut-throat competition that drives Windows development. Unlike the Windows platform, there were few enterprise sales to chase on the Mac, and its limited market share meant that growth happened deliberately and slowly.

Group Single-mindedness

Of course, not all big companies produce bad products, and not all small shops produce good ones. And it would be reasonable to think that a big company's repressive organizational structure is, at the worst, a kind of creative carcinogen—something that leaks into products quietly and does indiscreet damage, in a way the user would only begin to notice after constant use. But according to Walkin, a company that isn't conducive to thoughtful design leaves obvious markers on the face of its software. "There are companies that do purely visual design," he says—meaning fancy icons, glossy windows, and dialogue boxes—"and use that for interaction design. And it always produces bad results." Windows Vista, he says, is a case in point. "They hired this designer to re-make the interface, and she basically went and made things glossy in Photoshop," he says. "But there's been no attention paid to the interaction with that software. It was made without considering the user at all." He laughs. "I almost don't see how it could have been designed by anyone," he says of Vista.

The designers at Microsoft, he says, aren't actually culpable for the company's interactive downfalls; it's simply the byzantine structure of their product development that creates problem after problem. The more important a project, the more designers assigned to it, and in turn, the more agendas competing to shoe-horn features into the apps and make their mark. ("Microsoft hires tons and tons of designers—it's horrible," he says.) Nowhere is this more evident than Redmond's email app for the Mac platform, Entourage. "If you use the 'My Day' window in Entourage, it has buttons in that window that are extremely small," Walkin says. "If you're on a laptop with a track pad, good luck clicking those buttons," he says. "It's clear they didn't pay any attention to how the user experience works." (Figure 12–5 shows Entourage's "My Day" window.)

Figure 12–5. *Microsoft Entourage's nearly un-usable "My Day" window.*

The root problem is size without leadership. Walkin acknowledges that all organizations have their problems, but the larger the company, the more easily the end user's interests get lost in the shuffle. Echoing off-the-record comments of other engineers interviewed for this book, Walkin describes Microsoft's problem as a series of conflicts of interest. "There are managers of other teams, and people who aren't even in engineering trying to get a feature in a product," he says. Their motivations vary from careerist to truly well-intentioned, but the effect is the same. "They use their leverage to make changes, and it creates this weird power dynamic," he says. "And that causes the software to suffer."

"I put a lot of focus on trying to readjust the way things worked at Marketcircle so we wouldn't have these issues," Walkin says, of the feature-vetting process. While the company may not have suffered from the institutional bungling of a large firm like Microsoft, it was threatened by an opposite phenomenon: people in the company cared too much about the software. Marketing or salespeople could be eager to tout a new advantage over a competitor, or one of the top brass could be emotionally attached to a hard-won feature from a previous version. Walkin's challenge was to direct all that goodwill into creative energy, instead of letting discussions devolve into a power struggle. "I like a positive discussion," he says, "and I put tons of effort into making that productive. But you also have to stand your ground and clearly articulate these issues to stakeholders in the company. If there's someone in sales trying to get ideas in the app, you have to go explain to them that ideas can only go in after a vigorous design process," he says. "Part of my promotion to head [of user experience team] is that we now have a lot more control of design and marketing. We can go and do things without going and verifying with AJ."

In a sense, Walkin has introduced a pinch of absolutism into the company, and in doing so, he's helped change Marketcircle's chain of authority into something much more like Apple's. While Steve Jobs undeniably keeps a level power over his company that borders on despotic, he has given the constituent parts of Apple surprising autarchy. The aesthetic and functional lure of Apple's hardware, for example, comes from the mind of Senior Vice President of Industrial Design, Jonathan Ive, who is said to have enjoyed independence designing the original iMac, the click-wheel iPod, the Titanium PowerBook G4, and the iPhone. Credit for Cupertino's drool-worthy marketing and its world-class developer support are due to Phil Schiller, Senior Vice President of worldwide product marketing and one of Jobs' right-hand men. And as the *New York Times* noted in 2006, the wild success of the Apple store doesn't belong to Jobs, either: it's the product of former Target retailing executive Ron Johnson, who was given complete creative control to make Apple's stores "big and spacious, a physical embodiment of the Apple brand."[1]

In the same spirit, AJ retains veto power over Marketcircle, but his designers have earned a degree of independence that has worked to the benefit of Billings. Which is to say, they've earned AJ's trust—something that is increasingly difficult to do the larger a company gets. Nowhere is that more evident than Google, Walkin says. Though he has immense respect for the search giant's products ("they really get interaction design," he says), he notes that they are tentative about giving their visual designers real creative control. "Their apps are visually acceptable—Gmail, for instance, is nothing to look at— but usability-wise, they have it down," he says. "They have talented interaction designers, but have large institutional problems with respect to visual design. They're very focused on user testing there." Walkin tells the story of a colleague who worked as a visual designer at Google, but later quit in frustration. "I think he was doing an interface: the border of a window. Google made him test with users which thickness— two, three, four pixels—and which shade of 44 different shades of blue would be optimal," he says. "When you have an organization with distrust of visual designers to that extent, you can't really have a designer who has a vision, who makes an excellent design. Imagine if Apple did that with MobileMe—it would be terrible. You pretty much can't synthesize a coherent visual design language by user testing. That's impossible." In essence, Marketcircle has discovered the Apple model of interactive design. Call it "group single-mindedness": ideas float freely up the chain of command, and discussion happens across the breadth of the company. But ultimately, the creativity of many is funneled into the agenda of a small group of strong-willed decision-makers with a very personal vision about how software is supposed to work.

Marketcircle's principals are in no shortage of vision for Apple's software, too. "Back when we were developing Daylite, I fundamentally hated AppleScript," says AJ. "There

---

[1] http://www.nytimes.com/2006/05/19/technology/19apple.html?ex=1305691200&en=0a5d2e724d 58ac68&ei=5090

were limitations, and we had issues with it." The company explored other scripting languages, like Ruby and Python, but none had an easy hook into the Cocoa environment. Then AJ found F-script, which he calls a "phenomenal piece of work." The engineers used it for Daylite Mail Integration, the app's email plug-in. Then they figured out what else it could do.

Reverse Engineering Cocoa

F-script works on top of Mac OS X's Cocoa API, and is even more purely objective than Objective C itself. Although the latter simply introduces Smalltalk-like messaging into C, every item that is manipulated with F-script is treated as an object. The beauty of F-script, says Walkin, is that it supercharges Objective C's ability to do type introspection. "You can do reverse engineering in Cocoa applications to figure out how they work," he says, "so you can really figure out how to do certain functionality that [Apple] doesn't let you do." He's talking about the company's beloved Interface Builder, which he says is too stiff about some of its interaction design. Because Apple doesn't document the methods inside Interface Builder, and doesn't make them public, Walkin took it upon himself to look under the hood and fix his pet peeves. (See Figure 12–6.)

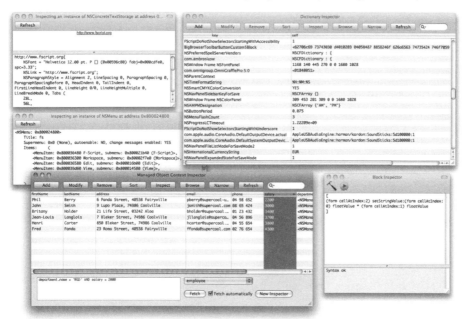

Figure 12–6. *Digging around in F-script.*

The result is a popular Interface Builder plug-in called BWToolkit that lets designers do things the normal builder kit doesn't allow. In some ways, BWToolkit is an outgrowth of his IndieHIG project: it documents all the UI elements that aren't in AppKit, and lets you alter them. (It's available for free under the BSD license via Walkin's web site).[2] One example of BWToolkit's features, he says, is the ability to set which panes inside an app resize when you resize the window. Mail and iTunes are examples. "Whenever you have two panes side by side, Apple has those panes resize proportionally. In every app in Leopard, like iTunes, when you resize a window, the source list window resizes, too."

But you don't want that, he says, because it ends up crunching the names of your playlists or sources. "In BWToolkit, you can specify what resizes and what doesn't. To do that without BWToolkit, you have to write a lot of code." Though BWToolkit is Walkin's pet project, he acknowledges that the engineers at Marketcircle helped him immensely when he began building it in the spring of 2008. "In fact, it's pretty much how I learned programming," he says.

What follows is one of BWToolkit's shorter Interface Builder additions, a transparent pop-up button cell.

```
//  BWTransparentPopUpButtonCell.m
//  BWToolkit
//
//  Created by Brandon Walkin (www.brandonwalkin.com)
//  All code is provided under the New BSD license.
//

#import "BWTransparentPopUpButtonCell.h"
#import "NSImage+BWAdditions.h"

static NSImage *popUpFillN, *popUpFillP, *popUpRightN, *popUpRightP, *popUpLeftN,
*popUpLeftP, *pullDownRightN, *pullDownRightP;
static NSColor *disabledColor, *enabledColor;

@interface NSCell (BWTPUBCPrivate)
- (NSDictionary *)_textAttributes;
@end

@interface BWTransparentPopUpButtonCell (BWTPUBCPrivate)
- (NSColor *)interiorColor;
@end

@implementation BWTransparentPopUpButtonCell

+ (void)initialize;
{
                NSBundle *bundle = [NSBundle
bundleForClass:[BWTransparentPopUpButtonCell class]];

                popUpFillN = [[NSImage alloc] initWithContentsOfFile:[bundle
pathForImageResource:@"TransparentPopUpFillN.tiff"]];
                popUpFillP = [[NSImage alloc] initWithContentsOfFile:[bundle
pathForImageResource:@"TransparentPopUpFillP.tiff"]];
                popUpRightN = [[NSImage alloc] initWithContentsOfFile:[bundle
pathForImageResource:@"TransparentPopUpRightN.tiff"]];
```

---

[2] http://brandonwalkin.com

```
                        popUpRightP = [[NSImage alloc] initWithContentsOfFile:[bundle
pathForImageResource:@"TransparentPopUpRightP.tiff"]];
                        popUpLeftN = [[NSImage alloc] initWithContentsOfFile:[bundle
pathForImageResource:@"TransparentPopUpLeftN.tiff"]];
                        popUpLeftP = [[NSImage alloc] initWithContentsOfFile:[bundle
pathForImageResource:@"TransparentPopUpLeftP.tiff"]];
                        pullDownRightN = [[NSImage alloc] initWithContentsOfFile:[bundle
pathForImageResource:@"TransparentPopUpPullDownRightN.tif"]];
                        pullDownRightP = [[NSImage alloc] initWithContentsOfFile:[bundle
pathForImageResource:@"TransparentPopUpPullDownRightP.tif"]];

                        enabledColor = [[NSColor whiteColor] retain];
                        disabledColor = [[NSColor colorWithCalibratedWhite:0.6 alpha:1]
retain];
}

- (void)drawBezelWithFrame:(NSRect)cellFrame inView:(NSView *)controlView
{
                        cellFrame.size.height = popUpFillN.size.height;

                        if ([self isHighlighted])
                        {
                                        if ([self pullsDown])
                                                        NSDrawThreePartImage(cellFrame,
popUpLeftP, popUpFillP, pullDownRightP, NO, NSCompositeSourceOver, 1, YES);
                                        else
                                                        NSDrawThreePartImage(cellFrame,
popUpLeftP, popUpFillP, popUpRightP, NO, NSCompositeSourceOver, 1, YES);
                        }
                        else
                        {
                    if ([self pullsDown])
                                                        NSDrawThreePartImage(cellFrame,
popUpLeftN, popUpFillN, pullDownRightN, NO, NSCompositeSourceOver, 1, YES);
                                        else
                                                        NSDrawThreePartImage(cellFrame,
popUpLeftN, popUpFillN, popUpRightN, NO, NSCompositeSourceOver, 1, YES);
                        }
}

- (void)drawImageWithFrame:(NSRect)cellFrame inView:(NSView *)controlView
{
                        NSImage *image = [self image];

                        if (image != nil)
                        {
                                        [image setScalesWhenResized:NO];
                                        if ([[image name]
isEqualToString:@"NSActionTemplate"])
                                                        [image setSize:NSMakeSize(10,10)];

                                        NSImage *newImage = image;

                                        if ([image isTemplate])
                                                        newImage = [image
bwTintedImageWithColor:[self interiorColor]];
```

```
                                        NSAffineTransform* xform = [NSAffineTransform
transform];

                                        [xform translateXBy:0.0 yBy:cellFrame.size.height];
                                            [xform scaleXBy:1.0 yBy:-1.0];
                                        [xform concat];

                                        [newImage drawInRect:[self
imageRectForBounds:cellFrame] fromRect:NSZeroRect operation:NSCompositeSourceOver
fraction:1];

                                        NSAffineTransform* xform2 = [NSAffineTransform
transform];

                                        [xform2 translateXBy:0.0 yBy:cellFrame.size.height];
                                        [xform2 scaleXBy:1.0 yBy:-1.0];
                                        [xform2 concat];
                        }
}

- (NSRect)imageRectForBounds:(NSRect)bounds;
{
        NSRect rect = [super imageRectForBounds:bounds];

                rect.origin.y += 3;

                if ([self imagePosition] == NSImageOnly || [self imagePosition] ==
NSImageOverlaps || [self imagePosition] == NSImageAbove || [self imagePosition] ==
NSImageBelow)
                {
                                rect.origin.x += 4;
                }
                else if ([self imagePosition] == NSImageRight)
                {
                                rect.origin.x += 3;
                }
                else if ([self imagePosition] == NSImageLeft || [self imagePosition]
== NSNoImage)
                {
                                rect.origin.x -= 1;
                }

        return rect;
}

- (NSRect)titleRectForBounds:(NSRect)cellFrame
{
        NSRect titleRect = [super titleRectForBounds:cellFrame];

                titleRect.origin.y -= 1;
                titleRect.origin.x -= 2;
                titleRect.size.width += 6;

                if ([self image] != nil)
                {
                                if ([self imagePosition] == NSImageOnly || [self
imagePosition] == NSImageOverlaps || [self imagePosition] == NSImageAbove || [self
imagePosition] == NSImageBelow)
```

```
                                        {

                                        }
                                        else if ([self imagePosition] == NSImageRight)
                                        {
                                                        if ([self alignment] ==
NSRightTextAlignment)

titleRect.origin.x -= 3;

                                        }
                                        else if ([self imagePosition] == NSImageLeft ||
[self imagePosition] == NSNoImage)
                                        {
                                        titleRect.origin.x += 2;
                                        }
                }

                return titleRect;
}

- (NSDictionary *)_textAttributes
{
                NSMutableDictionary *attributes = [[[NSMutableDictionary alloc] init]
autorelease];
                [attributes addEntriesFromDictionary:[super _textAttributes]];
                [attributes setObject:[NSFont systemFontOfSize:11]
forKey:NSFontAttributeName];
                [attributes setObject:[self interiorColor]
forKey:NSForegroundColorAttributeName];

                return attributes;
}

- (NSColor *)interiorColor
{
                NSColor *interiorColor;

                if ([self isEnabled])
                                interiorColor = enabledColor;
                else
                                interiorColor = disabledColor;

                return interiorColor;
}

- (NSControlSize)controlSize
{
        return NSSmallControlSize;
}

- (void)setControlSize:(NSControlSize)size
{

}

@end
```

Despite BWToolkit's additions, Walkin—like all of the developers in this book—praises Apple's IDE. "Apple has done a fantastic job. If you compare it to other apps that do interface visual development, it just doesn't even compare," from both a programming and interactive perspective.

Walkin compares it to Sketchflow (seen in Figure 12–7), a new prototyping feature in Microsoft's Expression design studio that he saw demonstrated by one of Microsoft's program managers at the MIX Web development conference in Las Vegas in the spring of 2009. "They're giving a presentation on it, and the guy drags a button onto the interface, and double-clicks it to change the title. He types in reasonable title, and pressed Enter." But the button isn't big enough for the text. "And then he says, 'Oh, the title was too long, I've got to enlarge the button.' On Interface Builder, the button would automatically resize," Walkin says. "Why wouldn't you want that? This is their new application!" he says, incredulous. "Speed is really important in a wire-framing application. It's important that every time I make a button, the button will resize for me."

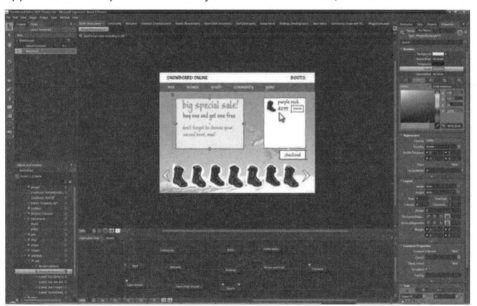

Figure 12–7. *Microsoft Sketchflow: be glad you don't develop with it.*

Another example, he says, is "a nice little optimization" in the iPhone SDK: drag and drop a label from the library onto a part of an interface that's black, and it turns white. "In any other program, that label would effectively become invisible," Walkin points out. Another crucial feature in Interface Builder, Walkin says, is Apple's suite-wide support for baseline guides, which help ensure that objects onscreen are aligned and spaced correctly. "Very rarely in other OSes do their baselines show up," he says. (The canvas

---

[3] http://videos.visitmix.com/MIX09/C01F

code that enables the guides appear in all of Apple's creative apps, which Walkin says is the reason he uses Keynote for prototyping.) "They're not gonna get tons of people complementing them on that feature," Walkin says, "but the Interface Builder team actually thought, 'Okay, let's get this really working.'"

The Sidebar Solution

It's clear that Apple's forethought inspired not only Walkin, but the entire Marketcircle team to do more with Billings 3. One example, says AJ, is the new sidebar that combines recurring billing with the "overdue clients" view. "We had this idea that came up: how do you see overdue clients? You could run a report, or add another window and hit a button and get a list," AJ says. But the real question, he recalls, became: What do you do with overdue clients? "If I have overdue clients, I want to send them statements," Jetha says. They considered adding a button for that, too, or a menu item that could run an "overdue client" feature. "But that's too deep, too hard to find," he says.

At the same time, they were chewing on another feature that customers were asking for: groupings for customers that could be enabled and disabled. "Our solution to all of this was to redo the sidebar," AJ says. "We took all those features and put them all into the pot, and out came this sidebar that has a red icon around overdue clients. Now when you mouse over an overdue amount, it becomes a button that you allows you to send them a statement." The new sidebar also let designers show invoices and payments more clearly, knocking down another customer request. "You can always slap in a new window, and off you go. But that's not the best way," says AJ.

Walkin says it's important to think about the most common user scenarios, and prioritize them. "I know every user is going to send an invoice at some point in the life of a project," he says, "and it's likely they will send multiple invoices. So I just design it for that. There's no reason they should have to select multiple slips." When Apple's Director of Software Technology Evangelism and User Interface Evangelist John Geleynse got on stage at WWDC 2009, it was the mouse-over invoicing button that he cited as one of Marketcircle's most elegant features. For Walkin, it encapsulated his career at Marketcircle; Geleynse was the primary contributor to the Apple HIG that he had monkeyed with to create IndieHIG, the site that got Marketcircle's attention in 2007. "It was a great feeling watching John Geleynse, who I highly respect, talking about Billings on stage," Walkin says.

At WWDC, another of Billings 3's innovations won particular admiration. "Some of the ADA judges asked us afterward what made us decide to build in the Client and Account button," AJ recalls. "We had this notion of seeing invoices and receipts in line, or at a higher level. We could have had a tab-based interface," he says. "We struggled. We explored. Finally we came to the solution of putting that button at the top to toggle between billing mode or account mode," he says. "It took weeks."

This time, though, the deliberation was less of a stalemate and more a result of due process. AJ says Marketcircle does very deep prototyping, but keeps their initial wireframes flexible so that they can drop in new ideas on the spot and get a reaction from the whole team. "A developer comes up with an idea, and then we'll have a meeting where ideas are presented. And since everything is in wireframe mode, things can be moved around easily," he says. (Walkin says he does detailed black-and-white outlines of the application in Keynote, "So you can figure out what goes where.") "It used to be that we Photoshopped [a prototype] for the final look, and then it would go off [for development]," says AJ. "Now our head of engineering, Mike, demands more wireframes, so we go deeper inside so we know, 'What happens in this case? What happens in that case?'" (A Billings 3 wireframe is shown in Figure 12–8.)

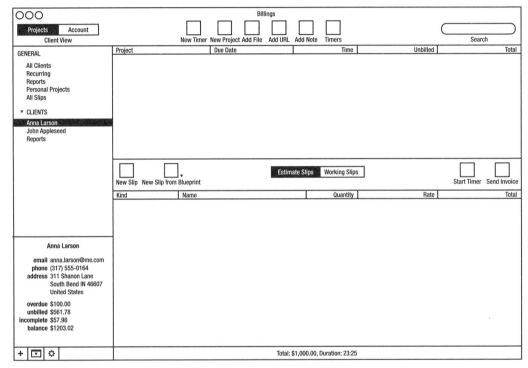

Figure 12–8. *Marketcircle keeps its early prototyping sparse and flexible.*

The obsessive preparations have made Billings 3 an archetypal example of how to make a simple program robust without making it ungainly. But it is also a cautionary tale in scheduling, and what can be lost when a release calendar takes priority over the product. "When we started Billings 3, we didn't want to make a new application—we didn't have time," says Walkin. The company's execs had given him two months to make its improvements. "I kinda knew that wasn't going to happen," he says. He approached the management team and told them he wanted to restructure the app's main window and how it worked, and make real improvements in interaction design instead of simple prettification. "Luckily, I was allowed to do that," he says. "We try and do an 18-month release cycle," AJ says, but acknowledges that "you need time to let it brew." (A progression of three Billings 3 prototypes is shown in Figures 12–9, 12–10 and 12–11.)

Figures 12–9. *A first of several progression of Billings 3 prototypes.*

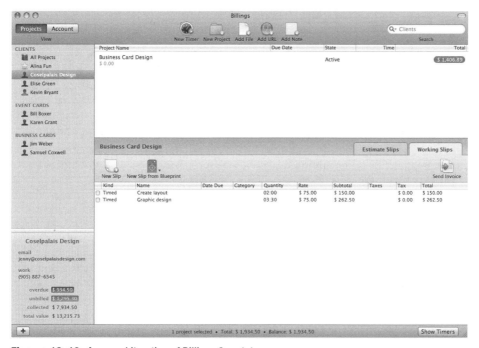

Figures 12–10. *A second iteration of Billings 3 prototypes.*

Figures 12–11. *A third iteration of Billings 3 prototypes.*

Enter the iPhone

As Marketcircle gets closer to releasing Billings Touch, an iPhone version of the app, the team has begun developing new software automation as well. "One of our engineers wrote a custom app that goes and downloads [mockup] images from a server and puts them full screen on an iPhone app." It can also do basic prototyping, Walkin says. "You can set it up to have certain hot rectangles on the screen, hit a certain rectangle, switch to another image—it's pretty cool, because you can actually see real workflows." (Other developers have said they use Ideo Labs' free LiveView desktop and iPhone apps for this same purpose, but Walkin contends that that app's presentation on the iPhone doesn't accurately reproduce colors. "It's too dark," he says.)

Billings Touch will be the company's second iPhone app; it released Daylite Touch at the end of June 2009, and won a MacWorld Best of Show award for it. "We've been working on Billings Touch for a number of months now," AJ says, "but we're running into problems: where we made assumptions that there'd be a natural fit, sometimes there's not." On Daylite Touch, for example, performing an action on the iPhone syncs it with the desktop version of Daylite. But because Billings is a single-user product, its mobile version is set up more as a standalone invoicing app that doesn't talk to the desktop version. "We're playing around with it right now: in our internal build, you sync [to iPhone] from the desktop," but not visa-versa, AJ says. "So far I'm thinking that it's better to do it from the desktop." (Figures 12–12 and 12–13, mockups of Billings Touch.)

Figure 12–12. *Billings Touch will be a full-featured, standalone invoicing app. Here is a mockup.*

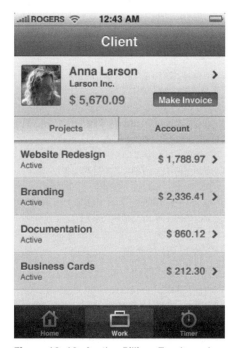

Figure 12–13. *Another Billings Touch mockup.*

At around $15.00 or $20.00, Walkin says Billings Touch will be one of the fully-functional iPhone apps that explores the upper price ceiling of the App Store. "The apps we're making having insane levels of functionality versus your basic iPhone app," he says. "Daylite Touch is basically a full-featured CRM for your phone." Setting the bar so high has made Marketcircle engineers question the wisdom of treating the iPhone like a full-fledged platform. "It's challenging to design [for the iPhone], in that the interactive paradigms on the iPhone were constructed for very simple applications that do one thing," he says. "They designed it for an app that looks at photos, for example, but not for an app that edits photos or compares photos," he says. Billings Touch will be "functionally equivalent" to Billings 3, he says, "and we're doing this with pretty basic interface. It's a fun challenge; it's what I like doing," he says, but admits it can be trying. "On the Mac, it's just easier; there are a lot more ways to fix problems." From a bottom-line perspective, Marketcircle is looking at a mobile version of Billings as a kind of leader to introduce Billings to a new group of more amateur users. "I'm sure when Billings Touch comes out, there will be a bump in sales [for the desktop version of Billings, which represents about 35 percent of Marketcircle's annual revenue]," says AJ.

Developing the iPhone app will ultimately have consequences for the desktop version of Billings, according to the team. Because Billings 3 requires users to keep their clients' contact information in Apple's Address Book, it stands to reason that the mobile version of the app will use the iPhone's native Address Book in the same way. "Some people have problems with that, because it requires you to have all your business contacts in your phone. If you want to have that distinction between friends—who you call often—and other people who you don't, then you won't want [clients] to appear in your phone," says Walkin. "We're looking at ways to decouple ourselves from Address Book while still maintaining the ability to import from it."

Developing a "power-user" app for the iPhone OS has made Marketcircle's designers intimately familiar with the limitations of the interface, but neither Jetha nor Walkin have any interest in designing for a competing platform. "In Daylite Touch, we used a tab bar at bottom of screen, just like the black bar at the bottom of the iPod app. We also had a nav bar at top of the window." But with the necessary window-title up top, Walkin says, "you can only really put two buttons at the top of the screen. If you need any more functionality that that on one screen, you need another bar below that, and visually that looks complicated," he says. "If you look at the Palm Pre, every app has it's own app-wide menu," Walkin says of the Sprint device released in June 2009. "For certain things that make context of the entire app, say like exporting a file, it makes sense to put that in an application menu." Still, Walkin says he's content to treat the iPhone's limitations as design challenges. "We're a Cocoa shop," he says. "It's what we do."

Chart the growth of that Cocoa shop against the development of Billings, and the importance of the company environment comes into stark relief. In very small dev shops, there's no problem; the engineers are also the business people, the marketers, and the PR department. When a company begins grows and its employees begin to specialize, it can be a struggle to keep the creatives feeling enfranchised. To let them lose hope is to deal a fatal blow to innovation. But the responsibility isn't entirely on the management to nurture its band of developers; instead, the onus is frequently on the developers to translate their ideas and opinions into saleable features. Sometimes, Walkin points out, the best way to do that is by building them.

Project Yellow Canary

"There were certain things we had to do under the radar," he says of Billings 3. "In the Send Invoice window, we had a pop-up. I always complained about that, because we had twenty invoice styles, so you'd have to go to the 'Preview' tab and click twenty items; there was no other way of previewing them. It was just insane. I really wasn't happy shipping Billings 3 with that feature," he says.

He decided to go underground. "Me and another developer started this project we called Yellow Canary, after one of the templates. I made thirty invoice icons in a couple nights, he went and coded this invoice gallery that lets you change the style. AJ had no idea this was going on," he says. "They had told us, 'You cannot make any changes to the send window,' because they knew that I would try to redesign everything," Walkin says. (The invoice gallery, Figure 12–14.)

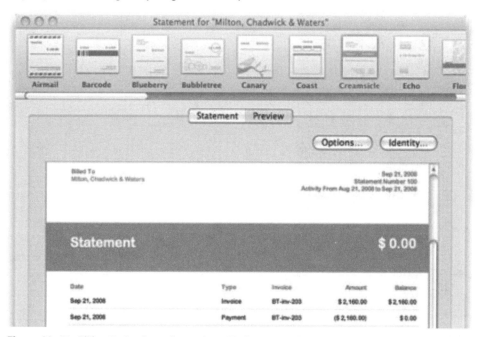

Figure 12–14. *Billing 3's invoice gallery, a.k.a., "Project Yellow Canary."*

Instead of censuring Walkin or reasserting his authority by throwing out the changes, AJ recognized a good thing when he saw it. ("I'm never against making something better, but I give people friction when something takes too much time," AJ says. "What made [Project Yellow Canary] okay was that there was no additional delay," he says.) The preview window stayed. Walkin believes that wouldn't have been possible in a team any larger than Marketcircle's. "There are people who argue that you can't make any effective institutional change. If you've seen the show 'The Wire,' that's what they argue in that show," he says, referencing the HBO cop drama. "The only effective change can be made on an individual basis. I just had to make that change with AJ. In a big company, you can't go up to the CEO and make a bunch of changes." He says he sees himself being frustrated by having to angle for power at a bigger company, where he wouldn't be allowed to control the user experience. "I do this for the design, for the end product," he says.

Software companies and Baltimore cop dramas aren't usually metaphorical bedfellows, but the comparison works—and it's not just about the depressing state of Canadian or American bureaucracies. In fact, it's more about the French—or at least, one Frenchman in particular. Emmanuel Levinas (pictured in Figure 12–15) was a 20th century Parisian philosopher who wrote a series of essays between called *Alterity and Transcendence*. He didn't talk about Baltimore, or invoicing software, or even F-script. Instead, he defined the titular concept, alterity, as the pursuit of "otherness"—or more specifically, the principle by which an individual can exchange his perspective for an opposite one.

Figure 12–15. *Emmanuel Levinas. What's this guy doing in an iPhone book? (Photo by Bracha L. Ettinger)*

The term "alterity" made somersaults through numerous academic disciplines before landing in the fourth season of "The Wire," when an impulsive narcotics cop named Prez gets fired and becomes an inner-city middle-school teacher. Seeing the desperate family lives of the kids he used to rough up on the corners, he becomes their advocate. Sometimes, the show seems to suggest, the best person for a job is the one whose relevant experience is on the opposite side of the given spectrum.

Project "Yellow Canary," then, was Marketcircle's "Prez" transition come full-circle: the company that began as a small team serving vertical markets with ho-hum interface design had ultimately become a place where engineers and designers were assuming a bigger workload—and risking their positions—just to improve the user experience.

During Daylite's development, AJ says, "We were all code monkeys, and so interface was a secondary thought. We got a lot of complaints. Usability was where the problem was. But I started getting more conscious about these things." Then the company got an ADA runner-up for Daylite 1, but AJ says that "interaction-wise there was much left to be desired." Once they hired Brandon Walkin's predecessor, Adam Baker, away from Apple, interaction design became a priority. "Especially after we started packing on features—it got out of hand," AJ says. "He started opening the door for us in terms of interface design; he had to really work on us, we were code people. But you really can't just do a veneer."

Now that design is in Walkin's hands, AJ has brought the company completely through that "door" of interface design. "I give him a lot of leeway—more than I would typically," AJ says of Walkin. Maybe that's an economic instinct: better usability equals more sales. Maybe it's the coders' conscientiousness, tackling interaction design with the same perfectionism. Whatever the case, Marketcircle's history seems to defy the old adage that tells us to "do what you know," and Billings 3 seems to suggest that novel territory isn't an obstacle, but an opportunity for thoughtful deliberation—and success.

Chapter 13

Upgrading

Developer Name: Marco Arment
Development Company: Marco Arment/Tumblr
Tags: Release Strategy; App Store; Iteration
URL: http://marco.org

The life of an app depends on more than just initial coding and design. It also relies on knowing how to handle the second act: upgrades, name-changes, spin-offs, price adjustments, and so on. And it means adapting to the fast-changing mores of the App Store.

To understand all that quizzical stuff, this chapter consults Marco Arment, lead developer of the blogging platform Tumblr, which claims 2 million users and one of the most innovative and user-friendly Web interfaces around. Arment is also author of the popular "read later" app Instapaper for the Web and iPhone (pictured in Figure 13–1). You can find more of his thoughts about the iPhone, the App Store and the Web at large at http://marco.org.

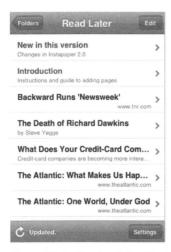

Figure 13–1. *The simplicity of Instapaper's UI belies its clever concept and execution.*

One question many of the developers in this book have pondered: do I charge for my upgrade? Do I charge for my app at all?

I just think totally free apps are just stupid these days. I don't mean put it in such harsh terms; I just don't think that people make that big of a distinction between free and 99 cents when they're browsing through the App Store for new things to download. I think those [price-points] are so close in people's minds that they're willing to take the 99-cent risk.

There still ends up being big difference in [sales] volume, but relatively, if you're going to release an app, I think releasing it for free is only something you do if the app is something that corresponds to a profitable web or desktop service. Zipcar's app is free, for example, because they don't need the app to make money; they make money through other means. So if you have that sort of external product that the app is kind of an ad for or kind of added-value for something else, then that's when you make a free app. I don't think it makes sense to have standalone functional app on the phone be free.

What about ad-supported apps like your free version of Instapaper?

I think ads are a total non-starter on the phone. I've partnered with The Deck for Instapaper Free, and that's the only partner I would've considered for ads. Almost every other ad partner is terrible.

That the ad quality is so bad on the iPhone is not the ad providers' fault—it's the advertisers', really. They're often serving things that are intrusive, or really cheapening, so you end up having this brilliantly designed app, and this lame movie trailer starts playing in the footer. I don't want that.

Another problem with advertising occurs when your app goes offline. West Coast people who don't spend a lot of their time underground like we do here [in New York] often don't realize that this can cause problems. An ad isn't necessarily going to be useful when you're constantly losing reception, and here you've devoted a good strip of your screen to that ad block—you're giving up valuable screen real estate for it, and it's not registering clicks.

I've ruled [ads] out as a primary monetization option for almost everybody. And if I didn't have a paid Pro version of Instapaper, I wouldn't have an ad-supported version. I put ads in my free version, not as a replacement for Pro, so I can make something off those people who are costing me money to run on the server end. That's really all those ads are for.

Are free upgrades a good idea? Or should you make users pay again? Let's use Exit Strategy NYC, featured in Chapter 6, as an example.

There are two options in the case of Exit Strategy NYC. Jonathan could make his version 2.0 an entirely separate app, and advertise this new subway app "with Exit

Strategy" data. But I think I'd still do the free upgrade route; from what I've seen, the new-sales numbers are much, much larger than the upgrade-sales numbers.

Part of the reason for this, I think, is that most people don't keep these apps. They try them out, and there's a high deletion rate. There are a few factors to consider with Exit Strategy NYC: one is that I would expect a high deletion rate for it in its current version. Once you know all your routine stops, you don't need the app that much anymore. You know the three stops that you actually use every day, and that's about all you need. For apps like that, upgrade policy becomes less relevant. Even if your second version is more useful, many users have deleted the first.

Another factor is that this is an app targeting New York, and people are less price sensitive here. When you're selling to markets like this one, you can get away with being more expensive than you could be somewhere else.

All that said, I'd reiterate that the free upgrade is the way to go—not because I don't think people wouldn't pay for version 2.0, but because I think there are so few people upgrading relative to the number of new buyers. The number of upgraders is so small, relatively, that it's not worth pissing them off. Those are the people that are going to be talking about the app to their friends.

Loren Brichter, who developed Tweetie 2 and is featured in Chapter 1, decided not to do a free upgrade. Yet Tweetie 2 still shot to the top of Apple's "top grossing list" when it went on sale. How is Tweetie 2 different from Exit Strategy NYC?

What Loren did with Tweetie 2 was indeed different. I think that the paid upgrade was fair because the app was already very, very popular. Most Twitter users who own iPhones and want a Twitter app on the iPhone already knew about Tweetie, and they've already decided that they use Twitter enough to buy this app instead of using a cheaper, or free, competitor. So I'm guessing that Loren's users are so dedicated that he would see a lot more upgrades than most apps.

What happens when the scope of your app changes with a second version, as with Exit Strategy NYC? Should Jonathan have changed the name and risked losing the benefit of SEO in the App Store, in the hopes of having a name that describes the app better?

I would never call what's in the App Store "SEO." He's right to have kept the name, but I think doing it for SEO reasons is looking at the issue the wrong way. It's hard to get found in the App Store. But [Jonathan] would be wrong to assume that people are finding it now. The question is: are people finding his app because of the App Store, or are they finding it because of external pressures, like people blogging about it or people talking about it? I think with a "real-life" and location-based app like his, you're going to get a lot of word of mouth—friends being like, "Hey, look at my iPhone, look at this cool app I have on it." I think very few people are finding that app in the App Store randomly, or through any sort of search characterization. The App Store is so cluttered with crap that it's really hard to search for anything by category or function. It's much easier to search for things when you know the name. It's the same thing on YouTube. No one searches YouTube like, "Oh, I'll just type in funny videos and see what I get." Of course not! There's just too much crap. So people go to YouTube when they want particular clip that they can search for.

The truth is, if you are not on the top of the App Store [lists], you're invisible—you don't exist. The Top list matters the most, and then staff picks, and the editorially selected ones, too. If [Instapaper] is on one of those, my sales will usually double or triple for the week that it's there. Then they go right back down.

Does the name of an app need to convey exactly what the app does?

That's a very hard choice. First of all, Exit Strategy NYC is a great name, so I don't think it would be worth giving up the name unless what the new version was doing didn't make any sense at all with the name. There might be a slight problem in that the words "Exit Strategy NYC" don't really tell you this is a subway mapping application. But he's going to have trouble competing for that "subway app customer anyway, because if he's priced at $3.00 already, he's not competing for the impulse buyers—and those are the people that actually need the title to say NYC Subway Map to make the purchase. If he is trying to compete for them, he's probably going to lose on price.

If he's already competing for a kind of premium market—a market for people who do a slight bit of research before buying anything—then he doesn't need to really worry that much about having the name say "subway" or worrying about App Store SEO; that's all irrelevant.

Do you think buyers have price "benchmarks" that developers should attend to?

Well, there is no one global answer for all apps; games in particular seem to command lower prices, for example, which is unfortunate because they take a lot more work. It seems that you can't launch a game for more than $3.00 unless your name begins with EA. So many times I'll read about some great game, and I'll go to buy it and I'll see it's 99 cents and I'll just feel bad; I would've paid more! So when we're talking about price, you've got to segment out the games, and that's a big segment of the market.

People talk a lot about downward pressure on prices, but I think the factors that contribute to that supposed downward pressure don't actually matter. Things like customer reviews and star ratings are a good example; they don't matter, not a bit. They don't affect sales whatsoever. Especially if you're not going for the impulse buyers, and if you're not trying to compete for the Top lists, then nothing in the App Store matters, because people usually already have decided, even before they click the App Store link on whatever blog they're reading, that they're going to buy the app.

When you hear people say that games need to cost x amount, or apps have to cost x amount, they're often saying that because they read some user review where somebody says, "Well this is great, but it really should cost less." But user reviews are just a bad sample; they do not represent the whole of user-ship at all. When people review apps, they are encouraged to be negative. The rate-on-delete dialogue really encourages negativity.

So reviews are skewed negatively in the App Store?

Yes, because there's no corresponding positive prompt. It'd be one thing if the third time you launched an app, Apple popped up the same dialogue that said, "Do you want to rate this app?" You know, some kind of corresponding equivalent that was in a positive context. But if you're deleting an app, you probably didn't like it very much, or you probably just no longer like it, or find it no longer useful. As soon as they added rate on delete, everybody's star ratings plummeted.

Point being, the people who are rating or commenting are very much a non-representative proportion of the population—most people, I think, are willing to pay more than those reviews suggest. Ask developers who actually sell something, they can tell you: "At this price I got this many sales, and at this [cheaper] price, I got this many more." The difference usually isn't massive. Many would tell you: "I haven't touched my price and I'm still doing fine."

What is the case to be made for apps over $5.00?

I know a lot of people who are still in the $5.00 to $10.00 range. PCalc [RPN Calculator, pictured in Figure 13–2] is a great example. From the very beginning, the developer launched at $10.00, just like I did with Instapaper; he's was like, "This is what I know it's worth, and I'm not budging on the price." I don't think he's ever even had a sale, and he didn't even have a free version until a few months ago. Still, he's doing fine! Because people who buy an advanced calculator app are probably somewhat careful buyers who are willing to pay $10.00. I mean think about it: $10.00 in the software world is still nothing.

The Top lists have also caused the [price] benchmarks to be set very strangely. The reason why we see so many 99 cent apps on the App Store is because people look at the Top lists and see everything there is 99 cents, so they think they have to price their app cheaply to succeed. But that's just wrong: people are willing to pay more than that. Maybe not 40 million of them, but you don't need 40 million downloads.

Here's what I mean: if you already have a limited audience, you can price [your app] higher and make up for the lack of volume you're going to get. Obviously you also have to consider your overhead, to make it worth it doing; sometimes you have to price it at a certain price or higher, or it just can't exist. That goes even for developer hobbyists, developers who have day jobs and do this in their free time; it's easy for them to think, "Well this doesn't really cost me anything for me to make, I'm doing it in my free time." But there's cost of time, opportunity costs, and sometimes cost of back-end support.

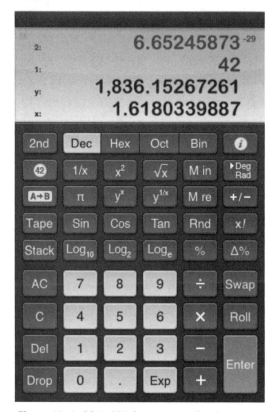

Figure 13–2. *PCalc RPN Calculator, by TLA Systems Ltd., debuted at $10.00 and has stayed at that price point. "People who buy an advanced calculator app are probably somewhat careful buyers," says Arment.*

You dropped the price of Instapaper Pro. What did you learn from that?

I dropped my price from $10.00 to $5.00 in late June [2009]. I had a feeling I was going to keep it at $5.00 permanently, but just in case I called it a sale in the event I wanted to go back up without too much flack. It ended up that my average per day is significantly higher—it's more than twice as high—so therefore, it's worth keeping the price at $5.00.

Why not go lower?

Well, it's important to remember how much relativism is going on here. When I went from $10.00 to $5.00, that got a lot of press and that was the biggest sales day I've ever had. Everyone who was used to the price at $10.00 said, "Oh my God, the price is cut in half from $10.00, it's a sale, jump on it!" Five dollars is still considered expensive for the App Store, but that didn't seem to matter to them—to them it was a sale. So if you start out high, you have that luxury of being able to incite more sales by a temporary reduction, at a price that is still a pretty good price for your product. But if you start at one or two bucks, you don't really have that ability.

Zach West, who is profiled in this book in Chapter 10, said he deliberately priced Prowl a little on the high end to cut out novice users who would flood him with support requests. Do you always want as many sales as possible if you're doing your own customer service?

Well, Instapaper is always a support-heavy app because it requires the installation of the bookmark. Installing the bookmark on the phone is a train-wreck of usability, it's really terrible, there's no good way to do it. There are two awful ways to do it, and you have to walk the users through creating the ["Save Now"] bookmark, then saving it, then editing it—I mean the process is just miserable.

It was really important that I got so much email in the beginning, because the users really did help me refine the instructions and the features and everything, and I made some really good documentation pages based on those emails. Finally I put up a note on my support page saying, "I'm sorry, but I can no longer answer emails about installing the bookmark, here's my best instructions," because most problems you just can't diagnose by email.

But in my case, at least, I have not really found that it has anything to do with price. Instapaper is a little weird because I have a free version, so I'm guessing most people try the free version first.

It's also worth noting that when I dropped the price to $5.00 I removed the mention of Instantpaper Free from the description of Instapaper Pro. Previously, I had a note in Pro that said in all caps, PLEASE TRY THE FREE VERSION FIRST. The situation I didn't want was people to buy Pro for $10.00 and then not being able to install the bookmark, since I can't give refunds. Right before I changed the price, the number of emails I was getting for the [bookmark installation] support issue had dropped to zero. And that's why I figured it was okay to remove the mention of free. As a result, I have very few people who bought Pro and who can't figure it out; maybe I get one a month. For whatever reason, Instapaper buyers do seem a little more technically inclined, and I am able to talk them through it.

Like a lot of iPhone apps, Instapaper has a desktop version. Should you build an iPhone companion app as a standalone?

Overwhelmingly yes. My initial assumption was that nobody would ever need to install [the Instapaper bookmark] on their iPhone, because they could sync it over from Safari on the desktop. I would always suggest that to people, and found that nobody was syncing their bookmarks.

Overall I was amazed at how many people do so much computing on the iPhone without using a computer. There are lots of people who write all their email on the phone, and it's become their primary computer—especially among less technical adults or teenagers who don't have their own computers but have an iPod Touch.

There are a lot of Windows people with iPhones too, so in the case of [developers] with Mac apps, the iPhone may be the only way to serve Windows customers. In that respect, it's a really good place to be if you want to sell software for money.

Why haven't we seen more apps like Prowl that use push notifications in a useful way?

Push has surprised me in a few ways. I was surprised by the complete lack of fanfare when it was turned on because people had been complaining for so long that it had been delayed—"We need push, I can't believe it's not out yet"—and when it came out, hardly anybody began using it.

I think people realized after they were given push that in most cases, they don't want it. It can actually get pretty annoying. Another thing that surprised me is that I had assumed before it came out that there was going to be this quick rush where one dominant app was going to replace text messaging with its own network, so it would be functionally equivalent but free. To the best of my knowledge, I don't think that's happened.

When iPhone first came out, there were a few missing links with MapKit; do you think push will evolve the same way?

No. I really think push is one of those things that people ask for, they think they want it, and if you give it to them, they quickly realize they don't want it. Users don't always consider the bad parts of what they're requesting. When people were asking for push notifications, they probably weren't considering that you could get overloaded with them, and they would constantly bother you about something insignificant. And a lot of people don't have the self control to limit the amount they receive, they go on information bingeing, and they want alerts for everything, and they end up with the most annoying phones in the world.

I feel the same way about how people abuse [RSS] feed readers. They subscribe to feeds that give them 1,000 unread articles a day, and they feel overloaded: "Oh God, I have too much to read!" Well, just delete some! But they don't make that leap sometimes. Twitter's falling into this trap now, with lists; people are saying they need lists of people so they can sort them and organize them. Just follow fewer people! Or create another account! It's not that hard!

So you can't assume your users have self-control?

Right! It's a very big problem. When I added feeds to Instapaper 2.0, I added folders, and I had this idea that I could add "starring" to folders like on Gmail. The idea was you could see other people other star articles, recommendations, shared folder lists, and everything else. At the same time, I thought, "Oh, I'll add some feeds, why not?"

Then I realized: this is going to be abused to hell. What I really wanted was a feature to give me something to read. But I thought I needed to limit it: the phone will only ever hold the most recent 250 articles, total. And its feed folder will only show the most recent 10 within itself. There's no way to get by this by paying more money or something like that—I'm talking about the Pro version, too—because that's not why I put the limits in place. I put limits in place to protect people from themselves. Because if you have a lot more feeds than that, updates will take forever to upload, they'll be loading all these things, not really reading, if the folders hold more than 10, they'll develop these huge backlogs when they ignore a site for a few weeks.

I have a similar feeling about "unread" indicators. People always ask me why I don't add an unread indicator to folders. No! I don't want to do that. People think they want that, but to me, an unread indicator indicates urgency and an obligation. It's not a simple status count. You see the red number, and it's like, "Uh-oh, I need to do something, something needs my attention!" And that's not what Instapaper is. It's specifically designed to remove that obligation from you, and to be no obligation.

Why didn't you make Instapaper for iPhone a mobile web site instead of an app?

Well, the main advantages would be for a web app you totally bypass the App Store. You could update quickly, anytime you want, and you could violate [Apple's] policies if you wanted.

But there are lots of problems building a web app for the iPhone. Before the iPhone 3GS and the 5th gen iPod Touch, you only had 128 megs of RAM, and WebKit is very heavy, very RAM-intensive. Because of that, there are a lot of things you just can't do if the base of your app is a web view, because it removes much of your usable RAM already. Now the web view does support canvas elements, which allow you to do a lot of fairly well accelerated calls. But still you're always going to get better C code, always. And there's always going to be capabilities with the phone that Apple will not have access to through JavaScript. Hardware's part of it—things like the accelerometer data, you can get some of it in JavaScript, but you couldn't do tilt scrolling, for instance. Another problem is that you can't really take a photo with the camera, and you can't do anything with the photo: you can't prompt user for a file to upload, for example. You also have very limited control over the keyboard, and which keyboard is shown, and what input is shown or not shown.

As far as a I know, I don't think you can do multi-thread JavaScript either. I don't think WebKit supports that yet.

If you're building a web app, there are also behaviors in WebKit that you can't override. I even hit some of them in the web view of my app. If you tap and hold a link, for example, the OS will pop up an action sheet asking you to copy, cancel, or open a new window. Or in the case of a web view, it'll just say copy or cancel. That's new to 3.0, but I can't disable that on my app. I have no control of that menu, and I'm not even notified when that shows up.

There are also all those little built-in browser features that you can't disable in your web app, too, like selection of text. If you have something that is technically a link, but you're using it for some image JavaScript thing, if someone taps and holds it, it's going to perform the copy action.

Or if someone leaves your app, they switch to something else, on a 3G with only 128 megs of RAM, when they come back, it'll be flushed out of memory. It'll have to be reloaded, but it doesn't necessarily notify you in the right way that it has reloaded. It's very strange.

Another problem occurs if you hit a JavaScript exception; mobile Safari will do what every other browser does when it hits an exception, it will just stop executing the JavaScript. No notification happens, and you can't catch the exception that easily— there's nothing you can do. The web app just stops working and nobody knows why.

Index

You Need the Companion eBook

Your purchase of this book entitles you to buy the companion PDF-version eBook for only $10. Take the weightless companion with you anywhere.

We believe this Apress title will prove so indispensable that you'll want to carry it with you everywhere, which is why we are offering the companion eBook (in PDF format) for $10 to customers who purchase this book now. Convenient and fully searchable, the PDF version of any content-rich, page-heavy Apress book makes a valuable addition to your programming library. You can easily find and copy code—or perform examples by quickly toggling between instructions and the application. Even simultaneously tackling a donut, diet soda, and complex code becomes simplified with hands-free eBooks!

Once you purchase your book, getting the $10 companion eBook is simple:

❶ Visit **www.apress.com/promo/tendollars/**.

❷ Complete a basic registration form to receive a randomly generated question about this title.

❸ Answer the question correctly in 60 seconds, and you will receive a promotional code to redeem for the $10.00 eBook.

233 Spring Street, New York, NY 10013

Offer valid through 4/10.